DEAR BILL AND JOHN,
DID YOU KNOW THAT ....?

Dear Bill and John
Did You Know That...?

David Spencer

Produced in association with

WORDS BY DESIGN

2 South View Lodge, Piggy Lane, Bicester OX26 6HT

www.wordsbydesign.co.uk

ISBN: 978-0-244-30528-4

To Bill Coughlan and John Curtis

Thanks for all of those countless emails

and vigorous debates

And to Doug Dennis

With great affection, and had the times been different,

then who knows?

And last but not least

to the late

John Granville Davis

A talented musician, a good friend,

and a bit of an enigma

CONTENTS

FOREWORD

I've never actually met John Curtis or Bill Coughlan in person. We do, however, share a background in army music. Both of these gentlemen served as army musicians, but are of an earlier generation to myself having served in infantry bands just after the end of the Second World War, while I didn't enlist until 1963. Neither man went on to make a career in army music, but later enjoyed great success, John achieving high office with the civil service, and Bill in the world of education. I first came into contact with John through a shared interest in military music, and our membership of the International Military Music Society. Over a period of months, John and I exchanged emails, and his long-standing and good friend, Bill, somehow came on-line to join us in our long, and often detailed correspondence. As both John and Bill are at the opposite end of the political spectrum to myself, and their knowledge of a large number of subjects, ranging from world history, international politics, and British social history, is considerable; I quickly realised that if I was going score any points, then I had to do my homework to avoid being shot down in flames. As these two gentlemen started to metaphorically beat me up, I racked my brains to come up with a subject where I knew without doubt that I had the upper hand; this book, or should I say letter, is the result. As I make no secret of my sexuality, both Bill and John were very aware of my history and of the various trials and tribulations of my past. It occurred to me that having no experience of my world, along with vast swathes of the rest of British society, they could perhaps learn something about the lives led by homosexuals since the days of Oscar Wilde, and who better to enlighten them than me? Having not been born at the time of many of the events portrayed in my letter to them both, I really have had to do my homework, while at the same time, I've been able to rewrite my own personal history in greater detail than ever before. While Bill and John are very real people, the names that I used could just as easily have been Dave and Mavis, or Kevin and Sharon. It's not the names that are important, but the story.

Oscar Wilde, and a Few Things That You May Not Know

Dear Bill and John,

The renewed interest in the Wilde affair caused by the stage play that you mentioned, gives me a good opportunity to talk about a subject that I know about from my own personal experience, and which gives me a great advantage over you both. You will never in your long lives have experienced what it was like for gay men like me, not so many years ago in the dark days prior to 1967. So here goes.

In this first section, I've used some excellent books as sources of reference. The most prominent being, 'Queer London' by Matt Houlbrouk, a fellow of Magdalen College, Oxford, and winner of the Longman History Today book of the year award.

With the legislation introduced in the 1885 amendment which criminalized any act of 'gross indecency' between men in 'public or private' and further complimented by the offence of 'indecency' under many local bye-laws, the 'state' effectively turned into criminals, at the stroke of a pen, a whole section of the British population whose only crime was to be 'different'. They were to be hounded at every turn by the police, and were to be kept under surveillance by plain-clothed detectives who infiltrated any place where gay men congregated; and where any infringement of the law would be noted and the men involved would be arrested and brought before the courts. The principal of an 'Englishman's home being his Castle' and therefore ' his private space' where the law did not intrude, only applied to the 'normal family man', but not the 'sexual deviant' of the homosexual world. On this subject, Houlbrook goes on to say:

> For queer men, these provisions had profound implications, for the law threatened to follow them into the intimate, prosaic, and ubiquitous spaces of everyday urban life. If they looked for partners in the street or park or simply had sex in their own home, they could be arrested, prosecuted, imprisoned for up to ten years, and – in certain cases – whipped. If they met friends in a cafe they could be caught up in a police raid, their names taken, and the venue closed. The formal technology of surveillance institutionalised and embodied by the law suggested that the British State was unwilling to tolerate any expression of male same-sex desire, physical contact, or social encounter. In all its erotic, affective, and social relations the queer body – and the spaces it inhabited – was a public body, was subject to the draconian force of law. De jure, the modern metropolis held no place for the queer.

It sounds more like a police state, rather than a country that prides itself on its principals of 'fair play' and calls itself a 'democracy'. Is it any wonder that I've said countless times over the years, that I have a good idea what it must have been like for the German Jew, living under the Nazi regime in the early days of Hitler's Reich. The Gestapo would have been proud of the tactics use by the British police on behalf of the State. I'll give you many instances of this repression over the coming pages, but now to continue.

1
The Public Schools

In a recent email, Bill, you said that sexual abuse was widespread in public schools and that was the reason why Wilde was subjected to such vitriol and hate by men of his own class once he was exposed. I was dubious about this, and decided to do some research using sources from published journals and books. And what I discovered confirmed my original thoughts. However, I think a more likely explanation, and I know this from my own experience, is that many adolescent boys who had gay sexual relationships were often filled with guilt and self-loathing afterwards. As they grew to maturity they transferred this self-loathing to a loathing and hate of homosexuals in general. I intend to cover this subject in much greater detail later in this letter. I'm sure, Bill, that you'll argue that as the boys involved were almost always of different ages, then the older boy was guilty of the abuse of the younger. I think that in this instance, that argument is totally out of context.

Homosexuality was indeed widespread in public schools, mostly between pupils, and in some cases, between pupils and masters. However, this sexual behaviour seems to have been almost always consensual. It's been said by various historians over the years that 'Homosexuality was officially denounced in the public school system, yet institutionally encouraged'. Wilde's crime was not so much that he'd had gay relationships, but that his affairs became public. And I guarantee, that the men who spewed the most hate and bile against Wilde, had themselves had numerous gay sexual encounters at their own public schools, and were in fact repressed homosexuals, not at all uncommon. I think that those who shouted the loudest were in fear of being accused of 'guilt by association,' and that the Liberal government of the time came down hard on Wilde to divert attention from their own homosexual adventures. W T Stead, in defence of Wilde at the time of his trial, said that 'If all the people from public schools who were guilty of Wilde's crimes were to be charged, then there would be a very surprising exodus from Harrow, Eton, Rugby, etc. A contemporary of Wilde's, Millard, made the same point about Oxford and Cambridge, saying, 'Poederism is as common as fornication and everyone knows it'. That's not to say that the public schools didn't make gay relationships as difficult as possible. In fact they did everything that they could to put obstacles in the way of boys to prevent it. However, boys being boys, when faced by authority and forbidden to do something, they always found a way around it. I think that the authorities who ran these schools realized the impossibility of controlling their pupils 24/7, and did what they could to control the 'evils' of homosexuality. It seems to have been a pretty dismal failure. Winchester College seems to have been a hot bed of homosexual activity. When Alfred Douglas went to the school aged thirteen in 1884, he embarked on a large number of affairs with different boys. One of the longest lasting was with a boy called John Gray. Gray later went on to have an affair with Oscar Wilde. Bosie was later to say about his time at Winchester that after the initial shock of finding all of this homosexual activity he, and I quote, said:

> I got used to the conditions, adapted myself to the standard of morality – or rather immorality – and enjoyed the whole thing immensely.

John Addington Symonds wrote the following about his own school, Harrow:

Every boy of good looks had a female name, and was recognised as either a public prostitute or as some bigger fellows 'bitch'. Bitch was the word in common usage to indicate a boy who yielded his person to a lover. The talk in the dormitories and studies was incredibly obscene. Here and there one could not avoid scenes of onanism, mutual masturbation, the sports of naked boys in bed together. There was no refinement, no sentiment, no passion; nothing but animal lust in these occurrences.

C S Lewis also wrote extensively about homosexuality at his public school, Wyvern. He says the younger, fey, and pretty boys, were described as 'tarts' while the older boys were known as 'bloods'. Many of the tarts would have more than one paramour, and these relationships usually had some permanence. The boys involved in these affairs had genuine affection for each other, and while no money ever passed between them, the older boys would do everything in their power to look after and protect the younger ones. There's no evidence, that I can find, of any younger boy being forced into an unwanted sexual relationship. Not only would sexual abuse have been highly dangerous for the perpetrator, but given the circumstances, totally unnecessary. Lewis goes on to say that the all of the boys would discuss the various liaisons, talking about, who had 'a case with', who, how often and where they would meet, and who had a photo of whom. Lewis, who had absolutely no inclination to gay sexual relationships himself, seems to have had only one complaint. It appears that he shared a room with one of the tart's, and was most put out when he had to vacate his room whenever the tarts boyfriend turned up for an hour or two of passion.

Of course it would be absurd to assume that every boy at every public school indulged in homosexual behaviour, far from it, and it will only have been practised by a small minority of boys. But there can be no doubt that every boy within these schools knew of, and accepted as the 'norm', the gay subculture within the school, as CS Lewis's acceptance seems to indicate. It also seems to have been an unwritten rule, almost a code that these matters were never discussed outside of the school by the boys, and never within earshot of a parent or adult. It wasn't so much a case of homosexuality being the crime. No, the crime was being found out, and when that happened the schools governor's retribution was terrible indeed.

There were also a number of cases of boys and masters also having affairs, but again, these seem to have been consensual. One of the most prominent of these involved the headmaster of Harrow, Dr Charles Vaughn, and a pupil. The boy was a friend of John Addington Symonds. Symonds, witnessed Vaughn caressing his friend as they were sitting together at a desk. There is speculation that Symonds was jealous of the affair which prompted him, once up at Oxford, to tell his tutor what he'd seen. The tutor, absolutely horrified, urged Symonds to tell his father, which he did. The father went to see Vaughn, and threatened him with exposure if he didn't immediately resign. Vaughn's wife even got down on her knees and appealed to the father to spare her husband, all to no avail. Vaughn resigned, but that wasn't the end of it. Vaughn was later offered the bishopric of Rochester and was again threatened with exposure if he accepted and so was forced to decline. Yet another life, one of countless thousands, completely ruined.

2
The Effect of the 1885
Labouchere Amendment

Prior to 1885, prosecution for homosexual offences were extremely rare. In fact most sexual acts between men were not illegal and so not subject to prosecution under the law. The one exception being 'sodomy', which by 1861 was punishable by life imprisonment. Prosecutions for sodomy were rare because the prosecution had to prove penetration, which was almost impossible. This all changed when the Labouchere amendment came into force, as it criminalised any sexual act between men either in private or public, and if convicted, the sentence at the discretion of the judge could be two year's imprisonment. Furthermore, there was a vague clause which allowed for the prosecution of anyone who 'played party to the commission of 'gross indecency'. This clause essentially served as a conspiracy charge, allowing for a broader pool of prosecutions. In other words, you didn't need to have carried out a sex act with another man as just the intention of doing so (importuning) would be enough to convict you. This vindictive peace of legislation, was rushed through in four minutes in the early hours of August 7, 1885, and would be on the statute books for the next 82 years, giving the authorities *carte blanche* to prosecute a group of men whose only crime was to be 'different from the norm'. Thousands of men would be prosecuted over the coming decades, their lives almost always irrevocably altered and in many cases destroyed. No one will ever know how many were driven to suicide during those years, but there must have been many, while those who tried to carry on with their lives were socially ostracised by an uncaring society who treated them with loathing and contempt; as something less than human. My own early years were to be blighted by my homosexuality, causing me deep unhappiness and profoundly affecting my psychological and physical health, the scars of which I carry with me to this day. Later in this article, I will go into greater detail of my early years, until the time came when like thousands of others in my position, I was finally able to break free and lead a normal life.

To sum up. I firmly believe that the 'gross indecency' law of 1885 was a state-sponsored stain on British justice, which can never be removed.

3
The Rent Boy Phenomena, Then and Now

A contemporary magazine of the 1880s complained loudly of the increase in male prostitution, saying that places such as the Quadrant, Fleet Street, Holborn, the Strand, etc. were thronged with men openly touting for business. They even claimed that pubs in the neighbourhood of Charing Cross had taken to putting notices in their windows saying, 'Beware of Sods!' It's interesting to note, though, that they were not so vocal in their condemnation of the huge number of female prostitutes that thronged the streets of the capital. There's a description in a recent biography of Oscar Wilde by Neil McKenna called 'The Secret Life of Oscar Wilde,' which I can highly recommend. The author has managed to uncover a large amount of new evidence on Wilde's actively gay, love life which seems to have been far more widespread than previously supposed. The book gives a wonderful description of a pub patronised by Wilde and other gay men, which was the nearest to a gay bar that existed at that time. The pub was called 'The Crown', in Charing Cross, and was patronised by a mixture of extremely good-looking and young, would-be artists and poets, with male prostitutes and servicemen looking to make some money on the side from the richer and older patrons. The place did a brisk trade, and Oscar met a young clerk by the name of Frederick Altaus there, probably introduced by Robbie Ross. Oscar and Frederick embarked on a love affair which lasted a number of months, but Oscar, as was usual with him, grew tired of it and moved on to his next 'conquest'. I've learned an awful lot about Ross from this book. From a wealthy background, he'd never attended a public school and had been tutored privately. He was also very well travelled, and by the time of his seventeenth birthday had already had a large number of gay sexual encounters, and was highly sophisticated sexually. Another incredible thing about him for his time, was that he had no hang-ups concerning his sexuality and was totally open about it. He even came out as gay to his mother, brother, and sister. He was either very brave, or extremely stupid, depending on your point of view.

One of my sources of research on gay life over a period of one hundred years is an excellent book written by Theo Aranson, entitled 'Prince Eddy and the homosexual underworld'. This is just one of a number of well researched books on the subject. It was said by a writer of the time, during the late 1880s, that there was almost as many male prostitutes in London as female. These young men were generally known as 'renters', and by far the largest group of 'part-time, or occasional' prostitutes were from the army or navy, something that I've know for many years. A large number of the young army men served with the numerous Cavalry regiments stationed in the capitol, with Hyde Park barracks being particularly busy. They were usually introduced to the life by older soldiers, corporals, or such, who would take them to well known pubs in the area and introduce them to prospective clients. Immaculately turned out with their scarlet tunics and pill-box hats, these young men were extremely popular and well paid for their services. Another way of contacting a soldier was to go into a newspaper shop near to a barracks, and buy a box of matches from the proprietor paying with a ten shilling note. This of course indicated what you were really looking for, and within a short while one of these young men would turn up and the deal would be negotiated. One of the great advantages for the client with going with a soldier was that you were safe from any kind of blackmail, as no young soldier would dare to draw attention to himself with the army authorities. The 1885 amendment quickly became known as the 'blackmailer's charter', and blackmail would become a common occurrence over the next eighty years. In his study on male prostitution and sexuality, Xavier Mayne wrote in his book, 'The Intersexes', that you couldn't walk through Hyde Park at night without falling over a large number of guardsmen entertaining their clients in the bushes. In fact, many of these encounters developed into long, and deeply affectionate relationships. In the same report, Mayne tells how one of the NCO's said to him, and I quote in full:

> When a young fellow joins, someone of us breaks him in and teaches him the trick; but there is little need of that as it seems to come naturally to almost every young man, so few have escaped the demoralization of schools or crowded homes. We then have no difficulty in passing him on to some gentleman who always pays us liberally for getting us a fresh young thing for him. Although we all do it for money, we also do it because we really like it, and if a gentleman gave us no money, we should do it all *the same*. Many of us are married, but that makes no difference except that we do not let gentlemen know it, because married men are not in request.

It seems from my reading that young, working-class men at the time, were far more relaxed about homosexuality than I ever realised, (their sexuality seems to have been almost interchangeable.) They were able to augment their meagre income, while having, if the report is correct and I have no reason to doubt it, a very pleasurable time. If you think about it logically, given the male physiology, it's impossible for a man to fake sexual arousal. If you're not aroused, or turned on as they say, then it's obvious to anyone with eyes to see. I would deduct from that, that these young men were gay and were more than happy to take part in these sexual encounters. When talking about this kind of casual homosexual behaviour by the various working class men who took part, I find that by far the easiest way to describe them is by using the term *bisexual*, to explain the way we view what they did, although I'm not sure that that's at all accurate. But it is the most *convenient term* to use, I find, to get some understanding. Take it from me, you cannot make someone gay, either you are, because of you genetic make up or you're not. I'm making this point before anyone puts on their 'the working classes being exploited by the toffs' hat, because in this particular case it just won't wash. There'll be much more on the subject later.

A Small Diversion

I'd like to divert from the issue of male prostitutes for one moment to tell the following story. It involves the army and is the story of an officer, a major, who had a lifelong relationship with his batman. I read a wonderful book many years ago written by the batman after the death of his lover due to old age. During the Second World War, the young eighteen-year-old conscripted soldier was made batman to a company commander. They both served in the the forerunner to my regiment, The Royal Warwickshire Regiment. It's unclear to me now how they both became involved in a sexual relationship, but it lasted throughout the war. This was incredibly dangerous for them both, but the fact that the young man was the Major's batman gave them a certain amount of camouflage, as, given his job, he would have spent a lot of time with his boss as part of his duties. This was a genuine love match, and as the war came to an end they discussed how they could stay together without drawing undue attention to themselves. The major, who was a wealthy man and owned a large house in the countryside, came up with an idea to solve the problem.

When they were both demobilised, the major offered his lover a job as his manservant in civvie street. The major's fellow officers thought this a good idea, of course not knowing the truth, to offer his 'loyal servant' a position in civilian life. This is exactly what they did and lived happily together for many years until the major died. To the outside world, he was merely a servant, while in private they were equals. Every time that I think of this story I feel incredibly sad. The fact that they were forced to live a lie, never being allowed to be their true selves, something that I, and thousands of others like me also had to endure, makes me more sad than angry. I just thought that I'd share that story with you. After the major's death, the servant wrote a book about their lives together. Sadly, I don't remember the title, as I'd love to get hold of a copy of this now long out of print book.

Now back to the world of male prostitutes in Victorian society.

In late Victorian England, the telegram was as common as the email is today, with thousands of them flying about the capital and major cities all over the country. However, many gentlemen seemed to send and receive more of these slips of paper than was normal. This was the start of a scandal that rocked the whole country, and was said to involve a high-ranking member of the royal family. In July 1889, a police constable was investigating a theft from the London Central Telegraph Office. During the investigation a fifteen-year-old telegraph boy called Thomas Swinscow was found to be in possession of fourteen shillings. This being the equivalent of several weeks wages, he immediately came under suspicion. Telegraph boys were forbidden from carrying their own money with them while on duty to prevent their money getting mixed up with cash taken from customers. When asked where the money had come from, young Swinscow, after hesitating for a while, admitted that he'd earned the money working in a gay brothel for a man called Charles Hammond.

The brothel was situated at 19, Cleveland street, which was just around the corner from the telegraph office. Swinscow had been recruited by a GPO clerk called Henry Newlove who then introduced him to Hammond. Newlove went on to introduce five more boys to the brothel owner who worked on a regular basis at the house. Number 19 had three full-time male prostitutes working there, but was also used as safe place of assignation where a man could take a young man picked up on the street for an hour or two in pleasant surroundings, for a fee of course. The telegraph boys were given a gold sovereign by their clients for their services. They then handed the money over to Hammond, who would give them four shillings in return. This was a considerable amount of money, and the boys were able to earn far more in half-an-hour with a client than they could earn in a month working for the GPO.

When the police arrived to arrest Newlove and the boys, they found they found the house in Cleveland street shuttered, and that Hammond had escaped after being tipped off by Newlove. Newlove, after his initial questioning about his recruiting the six telegraph boys, went to Hammond and told him to get out. Newlove was picked up the next day at his mother's house in Camden Town. Newlove, rightly miffed at having to carry the can, complained to the senior detective, a Chief Inspector Aberline, saying, 'I think it is hard that I should get into trouble while men in high places are allowed to walk free, 'What do you mean?' asked Aberline, puzzled. 'Why,' replied Newlove, 'Lord Arthur Somerset goes there regularly, as does the Earl of Euston and Colonel Jervois'. Alarm bells started to sound in the Chief Inspector's head when he heard those names. All of them were close to the Royal family, Somerset being an equerry to the Prince of Wales, and it's now certain that the prince himself, Prince Eddy, as he was known, was a regular at the Cleveland street address. The now closed house was put under surveillance, and a number of very prominent and wealthy men, some accompanied by young soldiers, arrived but quickly left when they realized that the house had been closed down. When sentenced, Newlove was only given four months hard labour, an incredibly light sentence, and the case against Hammond was quietly dropped. Some of the other boys involved were offered money to go to Australia and the USA. This all stank to high heaven. There was obviously a cover up by people in very high places, ring any bells? They failed, however, to take into account the press who got hold of the story and refused to let go. No Levesen then! Although the Cleveland Street scandal uncovered the telegraph boys involvement, the practice of telegraph boys augmenting their income by offering sex was widespread. Lord Alfred Douglas, 'Bosie', is said to have had many liaisons of this kind.

By far the most bizarre male brothels in London at the time was called 'The Hundred Guineas Club,' which was situated off Portland Place. Part gentleman's club, part brothel, it was a place open only to the seriously rich, gay man. The cost of membership, as the name implies, was one hundred guineas, or about three thousand pounds today, an absolute fortune in those days. I say bizarre, because the gentlemen and very attractive young male prostitutes were all required to dress in fashionable, women's clothes for the evening. The owner, a Mr Inslip, gave all of his boys girls' names which they had to use during the course of the evening's entertainment, such as Mary, Jane, or Evelyn. Apparently, it was all very genteel and sedate, that is, during the early part of the evening; Champagne, pleasant social discourse, albeit with an attractive young boy dressed as a girl sitting on your lap. This all changed at 2am when the lights were turned out and things really started to liven up. One of the boys who worked there at the time said that during the course of one night, 'I had sex with six different gentlemen and one of the other boys.' He then goes on to tell in detail just exactly what went on that night but I'll spare you the details. He also said that he was careful to appear at the club for only two nights a week, saying, and I quote: 'for fear of getting used up too soon'. This same prostitute also told of a party that he attended at a house in Grosvenor Square given by an earl where there were in attendance, three page boys (one of them black) and three gentlemen whose names could be found in *Debrett's Peerage*. I'm not going to pretend false shock at the goings-on at the club, and it most certainly would be false, but I just can't get the image of these bewhiskered Victorian gentlemen decked out in female finery out of my mind. And, purely from a personnel point of view, I can't understand the attraction, which seemed to be common then, of boys and men cavorting around in female attire. I would rather have thought that that defeated the object as the sexual attraction was male to male, so why bother?

I've purposely left until last, one more group of the gay prostitution world: the 'professional prostitute'. To these men, some of whom were aged about sixteen and looked like choirboys, while others were considerably older and could be described as 'rouged harlots', it was a business and nothing more. They all, however, shared one thing in common: they were street wise, cynical, and as hard as nails. Piccadilly and Piccadilly Circus were their favoured hunting grounds, and would remain that way for the next one hundred years. I remember talk of what was known as 'the meat rack' from my early days on the gay scene in the 1970s. The railed area around the statue of eros, was well known as the place to pick up rent-boys, who could be found draped over the railings looking out for perspective clients; hence the name meat rack. Cynical indeed. Xavier Mayne, who studied male prostitution at the time and reported the story told by the part time renters of the army, tells in detail the rituals employed between the client and prostitute.

The client would loiter outside a shop window for a while, or sit on a park bench. The perspective client would be approached by the prostitute who would catch his eye meaningfully and sit or stand next to him. The prostitute would start a conversation, talking of mundane things like the weather or the evening air. After a while, the prostitute would turn the conversation to more erotic matters, confirming to the client that he was indeed available. The client would then suggest that they take a walk together, heading towards the nearest public convenience where, if he so wished, the client could take a look at the prostitute's manhood, and if satisfied, they would head off to one of several private places. These could include thick parkland, the lodgings of the client or the prostitute, or even an hotel where the owner was prepared to turn a blind eye. The tariff, agreed beforehand, would be paid after the sexual encounter and would normally be between five and ten shillings. After it was all over, the two would go their separate ways never to meet again.

To give you an idea of how streetwise and savvy these boys were, Mayne talked to an angelic-looking boy with chestnut hair, pearly white teeth and blue eyes, called Wilson. This sixteen-year-old was an absolute magnet to the wealthy, older gay man, and he knew it. Wilson told Mayne, and I think that it's worth quoting in full:

> Do you think I ever let those old fellows have me? No fear, I know a game worth two of that. You see, I never bring them home with me, and in fact always affect the innocent – don't know where to go, living with my mother and father. If a gentleman is very pressing, I never consent to anything unless he asks me to accompany him to his house or chambers. Once got home with him I say, 'Now sir, what present are you going to make me?' The would-be client replies, 'Stop a bit my boy 'till we see how you please me.' 'No, I'll have it now' replies the boy, 'or I'll raise the house, you old sod. Do you think I'm a greenhorn? I want a fiver. Don't

I know only too well that little boys get only five or ten shillings once it's all over. But that won't do for me so shell out now, or there'll be a pretty good scandal.

Another boy, George Brown, was furious at only being offered five pounds by his rich client. He shouted, '*I could wipe my a*** with that. I mean to have a cool hundred.*' He went on to demand an IOU and threatened to go to the man's office the next day to collect the money. Brown then went on to demand the man's jewellery as security. The terrified man wrote the IOU and Brown was paid promptly the next day. As I said, as hard as nails, and Wilson was barely sixteen years old. It was not for nothing that the sexual offences bill of 1885 became known as the 'Blackmailers charter'. Wilson's threat to go to the man's office and cause trouble was nothing short of blackmail, and the use of blackmail over the next eighty years would become a widespread weapon, often ending in suicide.

Places that were regularly used by gay men and male prostitutes as a meeting place were the theatres and music-halls in and around central London. A favourite was the dress circle of the 'Alhambra Theatre' and a favourite haunt of the blackmailer. There were two of these men who worked together as a team. They were called James Burton and Frederick Atkins and were notorious blackmailers in late Victorian London. Frederick, the young and pretty one, would stroll around at the back of the circle looking for a likely victim. Once he'd picked his evening-suited target, who was obviously a man of means, he would zero in for the kill. He would take his chosen victim back to his rooms in Buckingham Palace Road, or better still, to a hotel room where a client was less likely to make a fuss. Burton would be following close behind. He'd then wait until he was sure that Freddy and the victim were in bed together, and then burst into the room. Feigning outrage, and pretending to be Frederick's uncle, he would demand a large sum of money in exchange for his silence. Getting hold of the victim's address gave Atkins and Burton opportunity to continue the blackmail indefinitely. These two were by no means the only blackmailers operating in London at the time and once they'd snared a victim then they'd bleed him dry or as was often the case, drive him to suicide.

In his book 'The Secret Life of Oscar Wilde', Neil McKenna says the following on the subject of the blackmail of gay men:

> Men who had sex with other men had to learn very quickly how to live with the blackmailers, or perish – literally, in some cases – at their hands. Those unfortunates unable to extricate themselves from the net of especially vicious and determined blackmailers would often be driven to insanity or suicide. John Addington Symonds gave a sobering account of how easy it was for a man to fall into the hands of some pretty fellow and have sex with him only to discover that he'd slept with a blackmailer. At that point, says Symonds, the subtlest methods of blackmailing began to be employed. Symonds continues: The miserable persecuted wretch, placed between the alternative of paying money down or of becoming socially impossible, losing a valued position, seeing dishonour bursting upon himself and family, pays, and still more he pays, the greedier becomes the vampire who sucks his life-blood, until at last there lies nothing else before him except total financial ruin or disgrace. Who will be astonished if the nerves of an individual in this position are not equal to the horrid strain? The nerves give way altogether; mental alienation set in; at last the wretch finds in a madhouse that repose which life would not afford him. Others terminate their unendurable situation by the desperate act of suicide.

Lord Alfred Douglas, while at Oxford became the victim of blackmail. Sadly, the details are lost, but whatever it was that the blackmailers had on him it was something of a very serious nature, far more serious than was the normal reasons for blackmail. Bosie turned to Oscar Wilde for help. Wilde employed a private detective who contacted the blackmailer(s) and they were paid off with £100. This detective, who'd worked for Wilde on many occasions, was so horrified by what he discovered, that he urged Oscar to cut all ties with Alfred Douglas forever. Both Oscar and Bosie used attractive, young working-class (known as 'rough trade') rent boys on very many occasions. Indeed they were known to go out together in search of this type of rent boy and couldn't seem to get enough of them. Oscar was very well aware of the dangers of blackmail from these young men and fell victim to it himself, but that in no way seemed to phase him. Believe it or not, one of Oscar's favourites, and regular bed partner, was the angelic-looking Freddie Atkins, of the notorious blackmailing duo mentioned earlier, Frederick Atkins and James Burton. Oscar seems to have had a soft spot for Freddie, and to have genuinely liked these young, seductive rogues. He likened it to 'feasting with panthers'.

Blackmail, however, is yet another indictment of the Labouchere amendment, which quickly became known as the 'blackmailers charter'. The minimum sentence for blackmail was seven years' imprisonment, but the blackmailer knew full well that by blackmailing a homosexual they ran almost no risk of ever being charged. And although Wilde seems to have made light of it, very few gay men would risk going to the police, knowing that he himself was laying himself open to criminal charges alongside his blackmailers. Not only that of course, but by standing up in a court of law he would be exposing his homosexuality to the world, something that very few men would ever have been brave enough to do. It also seems that the police actively encouraged the blackmailers as they saw them as a useful source of information. After all, it was argued, the victims were only 'queers' and deserved all they got. Is it any wonder, therefore, Bill and John, that I get so angry at the injustice of this pernicious, vindictive little amendment?

4

The Dilly Boys

Earlier in this letter I said that I knew little about the seedier side of male prostitution, but I'm now more able to throw some light on the subject of the rent boys of Piccadilly. Like most gay men in the 70s, I was aware of the 'famous' rent boys who operated in and around Piccadilly Circus, but knew nothing about them. In 1973, a South African called Mervyn Harris published a book about these boys. Harris had spent many months following them, and talking to them as they went about their business. They grew to know and trust him, and he came particularly close to six of them. The boys all shared one thing in common. They varied in age from fifteen to twenty-three, were all working class, poorly educated, and almost all of them had run away from home often after fighting with their father's. Many came from Ireland and Scotland and had been lured to the bright lights of the West End. They were quickly forced to realize that the streets weren't paved with gold; when cold, hungry, and almost penniless, they were forced to see their true situation. Very few of these boys are what I would call gay in the true sense of the word, and unlike the part time rent of the East End or armed forces, they drifted into it as a means of survival. They could usually be found in and around Piccadilly Circus and often congregated in the many amusement arcades where they could easily be picked up. Here is what Harris says about the way these boys were introduced into the lifestyle:

The peer group is an important pathway of recruitment to the ranks of male prostitution. It is this channel through which many boys learn about the phenomenon and the fact that there are other boys engaged in this activity makes it easier for newcomers to accept. A boy is told by a friend or an acquaintance that it as an easy way of earning money and having a 'good time'. He will be informed where to go and given elementary advice on how to behave and the approach he should adopt. The knowledge that there is a set of norms and a code with members who carry it out is a vital form of comfort and solidarity to the new recruit in the initial stages.

Harris points out though that these boys were never forced into this activity, and were able to accept or reject the offer put to them by a potential client. Apparently many of them had 'regulars' who gave them a warm place to stay for a few nights, but most of them shunned away from any client who became too attached to them. On rare occasions a boy would be picked up by a rich client, kitted out in the latest fashions, and sometimes even be taken away on holiday. Viewed as some kind of a trophy I suppose. Although, they seemed to have quickly tired of 'the good life,' and it wasn't long before they drifted back to their usual haunts on the dilly. The usual fee seems to have been five pounds at that time, and they were very particular of what they would, and would not do. Oral sex was the norm for most of them, and they seem to have been prepared to take the submissive roll in intercourse, although that may have cost extra. (I presume that they would have been incapable of taking the dominant role, although I can't be sure.) From what I've read about these boys, they seemed to have been totally detached from the whole sexual experience and were not particularly 'turned on'. They simply saw it as a means of putting some warm food into their bellies.

Harris tells an interesting story about a Scottish boy called Jamie. He'd arrived late one night in Euston Station and in quick succession was approached by two different men. They offered him a bed for the night, telling him what they expected in return. He turned them down flat. This so frightened the boy that he went straight back to Scotland. However, the seed had been planted in his mind and he could see a way of making a living. A few months later, he returned to London and went on the game. Harris also mentions a number of boys who were picked up by East End gangsters. He must be referring to the Kray twins. I don't know if you're aware, but one of the Krays was gay and had a succession of rent boys. This of course, had unique dangers all of its own.

I'm sorry if I seem cold and matter of fact in reporting this part of the letter but I'm afraid that I can't make light of something that has no lightness to offer. I should say though, that at the time that the book was written very few of these young men seemed to have been doing it to feed some kind of addiction as is usually the case today. Harris goes on to say the following:

> The problem of being homeless and rootless is not by any means exclusive to boys in the West End of London, but homelessness does accentuate their difficulties and in many instances is the factor propelling boys to take up male prostitution. Payment may only be a bed for the night and later many boys may only 'score for a pad' and, perhaps a meal.

It seems to have been rare for a boy to be arrested by the police for prostitution. It seems that as they were mostly under the age of twenty-one, the then legal age of homosexual consent, they were regarded by the authorities as victims of abuse, or that they'd been 'led on' by their clients. They did, however fall foul of the law in various other ways. Loitering and vagrancy were common as were arrests for petty crimes such as shoplifting or even bag snatching. Many of them spent time in Borstals and remand homes, and some even ended up in main stream jails. By the time these boys were about twenty-three their days of being 'dilly boys' usually came to an end. In conclusion, Harris goes on to say, and should have the last word as follows:

> The boys mentioned in this book who were active as prostitutes at the time of my research have, except for three who are still on the game, all left the ranks of the male hustler. Some have adapted more quickly than others to a new way of life while a few are still suspended in a sort of no-man's-land, rootless and adrift. Two of the boys are serving terms of imprisonment for breaking and entering and by the time their sentences are over will have spent nearly four of the past six years in prison. Three of the boys have left the West End and returned to their lives in the provinces. For those who remain in the area there is a strong possibility that they may drift into one of the other deviant activities, especially drugs. Two of the boys moved into the field of hard drugs and have become heroin addicts, one of whom is constantly in hospital for treatment. He later continues, 'The rest of the boys have all re-entered the straight world and taken jobs as manual workers, a storeman in a warehouse, and one has started a small business with a friend doing odd jobs and repair work. Three of the boys have got married and one of them has two children although he is not yet twenty-one.

I'm pleased to have been able to throw some light on the far darker side of male prostitution as it was in the 60s, and have to admit that I've learned a lot myself in the process.

I've spent a great deal of time talking about the varied number and types of rent boys operating in the capital during Victorian and Edwardian times, and now in the 60s and 70s. But what of today? The world of the gay male prostitute in the twenty-first century is slick, high-tech, and supremely sophisticated.

The young gay men who today prefer to be called 'escorts' rather than rent boys, are on the game to make as much money as possible during their rather short, professional career. It's not force of circumstances that takes them down the road of prostitution, rather the chance to make a great deal money in a very lucrative market; it's a business, no more or less. The clients of these boys have no need to fear blackmail, in fact one of the rules in the rent boy manual of 'best practice', is that discretion must be assured. This does sometimes go horribly wrong though for the client who has a high profile in society. There have been a number of cases over recent years of politicians and the like who have been shopped to the tabloid press by their chosen escort, usually for a very large sum of money. I suspect that the rent boy who does this is looking to take early retirement. This behaviour is the exception though. If you think about it logically, any rent boy who behaved like that would instantly go out of business, as previous clients wouldn't ever go back, and prospective clients would avoid them like the plague. I keep using the words business, and early retirement on purpose.

The one thing that has not changed since Wilde's day is that these professional rent boys view their clients from a cold, business-like perspective. They are not their friends. If I were a man who used gay escorts, and I'm not, I would follow this rule of thumb by asking myself the following question, as follows: 'Would this lad be rolling about naked in bed with me if I wasn't paying him handsomely for the privilege'? If you can answer that question honestly by saying no, then you should be OK. I get the impression that too many middle-aged men see their favourite rent boy as being their friend and best buddy, and even go so far as to kid themselves that 'he fancies me really'. He doesn't. I refuse to take any kind of moral stand on this subject as that would make me the worst kind of hypocrite. I'm in the very fortunate position of never having to resort to using a prostitute. Martin and I have been deeply in love with each other for forty years and have never felt the need to look elsewhere for sex. If my circumstances had been different, however, I wouldn't hesitate to use an escort from time to time. As we get older, and our looks fade, the likelihood of sexual encounters diminish to. That's something that the attractive, young, gay man having a ball in the various gay bars and clubs with numerous sexual partners falling over themselves to get their hands on him, would prefer not to think about. You must remember that Martin and I are a 'minority within a minority.'

Yesterday afternoon, in the interests of research you understand (honest), I went on to the internet and googled 'Gay Escorts London'. The results came as no surprise to me as it was as I'd expected. There were page after page of websites advertising the sexual services of gay escorts. Choosing the one at the very top of the page, I clicked onto a website called 'Black Tie Affairs'. The very name suggests quality and a first-class service. I wasn't disappointed as this high gloss, slick, and highly professional website appeared. My first reaction was to ask how much it cost to advertise yourself on this site. Staring at me from the screen, were pages of professionally taken photographs of the young men advertising their services, each with a brief profile. There's a vast range of different types of young men, enough to satisfy most tastes and preferences, from the beautiful, fey type, who wouldn't have been out of place sitting on the lap of a Victorian gentleman's lap in the 'One Hundred Guineas club'; to the more masculine and muscular type, with the obligatory tattoo, whom you could expect to be plying his trade outside of Hyde

Park Barracks in Wilde's time. In fact many of these young men say on their profile something like, for instance, 'Damien, ex-public school boy, or Gary, ex-military man.' This to indicate to potential clients their backgrounds and to indicate that you'll get a plummy accent, with the one, if that's what you prefer, or the more working-class accent if you're into the rougher, more earthy type. When you've chosen your favourite, click on the relevant photo, and you'll be given a much more detailed profile of your choice. This will tell you what services they offer. For instance whether they're prepared to visit you at your home or hotel, (they usually are but expect you to pay the travel expenses), or whether you have to go to them. They always give their age, anything from eighteen, a minimum legal requirement, to their late twenties, and will spell out what services they can offer, which is usually a pretty extensive list. If you like what you see, then all of their contact details are provided so that you can arrange a meeting time and place, and if you're really rich and energetic enough, then you can even ask for an all night session. Some even give their hours of business. The one thing that they don't tell you, is just how much these delights are going to set you back. That's discussed after you make contact, but do not expect it to be cheap! It's all very slick and professional, with even a FAQ page both for the client, and the escort, where things like safe sexual practices, hygiene, and safety and security are all mentioned. As I said, slick, glossy, highly professional, but utterly soulless. If you're looking for warmth, love, and affection, then you won't find it here.

5
And for the Vast Majority?

But what about the ordinary gay man, who could neither afford to use a prostitute or had no inclination to do so; in other words, the vast majority? Life changed very little in the years between 1885 and 1967 for gay men but a gay underground culture flourished. The absolute Mecca for gay life between the two world wars and beyond, was of course London. If by enacting the Labouchere amendment in 1885 the authorities hoped to drive homosexuals underground and out of public life for good, and by God they tried, they were greatly mistaken and underestimated the capacity for human beings to adapt to different sets of circumstances.

In 1916, a young, working-class student called Robert Hutton walked the streets of London's West end. He was absolutely captivated and fell deeply in love with the thriving, bustling metropolis. He said the following:

> Men in uniform, hucksters, prostitutes and men like myself, killing time and enjoying the crowds, jostled and strolled from the pavilion to Leicester square and back again ... When dusk fell a feeling of restlessness and excitement crept over me. Like generations before, and after him, young, gay men were drawn to the lure of the lights and bustling activity in and around the West End of London. Young men living in the dull provinces of England, longed to escape to the bright lights and relative anonymity of the capital.

Hutton went on to say:

> Some day I promised myself I would stay as long as I
> liked and mingle with the crowds instead of being an ...
> onlooker ... I would have liked to get into conversation
> with one or other of the young men in uniform and once
> or twice, I tried it, but did not get much response. They
> were looking for something and in a vague way so was I.
> I hoped that some day I might meet someone who felt
> the same way.

Later, the young Hutton was to meet a man who felt the same way. While browsing at a book stall in Victoria station he caught the eye of a well-dressed man of about thirty-five. Instinctively, they both recognised each other as being of the same mind, and they fell into conversation. They took a stroll into Belgrave square and had sex amongst the trees. After this all too brief sexual encounter, Hutton said:

> It was as if a curtain had been drawn back ... I could
> clearly see what had partially been obscured before ...
> this was what ... I had been looking for ... I knew now ...
> that other people ... felt the same way as I did. I was no
> longer alone.

Do you know, Bill and John, that's exactly the same as I felt on first entering the, 'gay scene', in 1975. No longer alone.

Hutton seems to have spent the rest of his life in the capital and was to be imprisoned twice for 'homosexual offences' (I'll go into far greater detail on this comment later in the article). I always feel that one of the saddest aspects of gay life prior to 1967, was the transient, anonymous sexual encounters that took place in public toilets and parks up and down the country. As encounters such as this were forever being reported in bold, hysterical headlines in the press, the general public started to view homosexuals as dirty, sick perverts, who had to have grubby sexual encounters in public toilets. This stigma was to stick to gay men for generations, and it was this widely held view that was to affect me throughout my early life.

But where else could they go? The West End was an ideal cruising ground for gay men. Bustling with life and full of glittering shop windows, where a young man could linger, pretending to gaze at the varied contents without drawing any undue attention to himself. This was a well known way for two men to size each other up and I don't mean that literally. Initially, while strolling along the busy streets, men would make eye contact with each other, a difficult to describe knowing look, an instinct perhaps, that indicated that they were interested in each other sexually. This would be the start of an elaborate game. Once the mutual interest was confirmed, with neither man uttering a single word, they would stand in front of one of the large, department store windows pretending to eye the display. From then on it was easy to get into conversation, one often asking for a light for a cigarette as an opening gambit. They could then stroll away together like old friends and head for the nearest, private enclosed space. This was very often one of the many public conveniences dotted all over the West End, where, unobserved (hopefully for them), they could slip into a cubicle for a brief sexual encounter. This was known as 'cottaging'. I don't know how that name came about but it certainly goes back to Wilde's day. In the 1930s someone published a map (I've seen a copy), of every cottage in the West End marked in green ink. The cottages were often set back off the road, were usually dark with barely any lighting and therefore ideal for clandestine sexual activity. But these men were playing a dangerous game. The police were very aware of these illegal activities and often kept the cottages under observation, waiting to pounce on the unwary, which they did night after night, with often devastating consequences for the men involved. This didn't seem to deter the gay men, from all classes, who used these places on a regular basis as a place to meet other like minded-men. The older and more experienced hands at the game always advised newcomers on the rules of the game. Never linger for long outside a convenience as this would bring you to the attention of the police, and after a short while, move on to the next nearest cottage. Keep constantly on the move and don't draw attention to yourself, and never be seen going in and out of the same place on a regular basis, seems to have been the message. Many of these places also had a particular type of clientèle depending on the location. The conveniences at Piccadilly Circus and Victoria tube stations were another popular meeting place. In the 1950s, there were a huge number of arrests of men in the London financial centre, particularly at Bank, and Blackfriars tube stations. Most of those arrested were bank clerks, but there were also stockbrokers, businessmen, and solicitors. This activity went on not at night as you would expect, but during the lunch hour and early evening. It should be remembered that many of the men involved in cottaging were married with wives and children waiting for them at home in suburbia.

The East End had a large number of conveniences which were heavily used by predominantly working-class males who lived within the local districts. During my research I came across an amusing story. One of the men involved in cottaging in the 1930s, and an old hand at the game, told how he always had two carrier bags with him when he went cottaging. If he met someone inside who was willing to join him, on entering the cubicle, he would get his partner to put one leg into each bag. Apparently, when the police entered the toilet they would stoop down and look under the door. If they saw two pairs of legs, then the door would be broken down and occupants would be arrested. This chap's idea was that the police came in and looked under the door they would only see one pair of legs and two carrier bags. Whether or not the ruse worked I've no idea.

The LCC were also very aware of their public conveniences being used for purposes other than those intended and during the 1930s, demolished a great many of the old Victorian public toilets, replacing them with modern, well-lit conveniences. These new places always had brilliant white tiles. Believe it or not, the idea behind this was that gay men would never use white-tiled toilets for immoral purposes, as they were put off by the bright, sparkling whiteness of the tiles. No, I don't get it either. Perhaps the thinking was that the 'queers', being dirty perverts, would be deterred by the pristine, clinical atmosphere. Who knows?

Cottaging was to continue as a way for homosexuals to meet each other for casual sex well into the 1980s, and may well continue in some form or another to this day. Personally, I've never been able to understand why men would want to meet inside a public toilet for sex. The thought of going to a dirty, damp, cubicle for loveless sex leaves me cold. But then again, when I was at last able to come onto the gay scene in the mid-70s, cottaging was largely redundant as there were many gay pubs, bars, and clubs, a lot of them exclusively gay, where men could meet each other and openly socialise. So perhaps I shouldn't be so quick to criticize these men who inhabited a very hostile, hate-filled world. When you think of the huge risks that these men took, simply for an almost adolescent, schoolboy grope, you have to ask if it was worth the cost if discovered.

I've often asked gay men of my generation and of earlier generations who regularly used public toilets why, given the danger, they went to these places so often, because we shouldn't forget that it wasn't just the police that they had to fear, but violent attack if they tried to 'pick up' the wrong person. I was surprised to be given a similar answer by different men, and at different times. They often said that it was the very danger of the exercise that made it so exciting: bizarre!

Cottaging was by no means the only way that gay men could meet. The two men mentioned at the start of this section could just as easily headed to one of the many parks and open spaces abundant in London, such as Hyde Park and Clapham common. This was slightly less dangerous, as the police were unable to keep their eyes on so many large areas of parkland. But there were other eyes constantly on the look out for suspicious behaviour. Local councils employed park keepers who, very well aware of what was going on were constantly on the look out. There were many other agencies too, like the religious and public morality groups who were concerned about prostitution and the lowering of moral standards. These groups carried a lot of clout within society and their suggestions on how best to curb the outrageous moral depravity that they saw all around them were listened to and enforced.

The Law Society in the 1950s – yes, the 1950s – defined the 'queer' as

> a potent challenge to normative domesticity: an attack on marriage, a barrier to demographic stability, and a threat to the nation's youth. This was an evil that the state could not tolerate.

'An evil that the state could not tolerate' – sounds like something written a few short years before by one of the most evil regimes in the history of mankind, and the kind of claptrap that could have been penned by Heinrich Himmler. To me, the irony of it all is that this country, only five years previously had fought a long and bloody war against such attitudes.

But gay men were by no means the only groups of people to use these places though. Because of overcrowded living conditions and a total lack of privacy, the parks were an ideal place to go for a young, heterosexual couple who wanted to indulge in forbidden sexual behaviour. It's ironic that two groups of very different people, both gay and straight, could be found in the same place at the same time, indulging in sexual contact of one type or another. There was also another ever present danger for gay men, violent attack and robbery. These men were a very easy target for anyone intent on robbing them, as the robbers knew that the victim was unlikely to report the attack to the police. Too many awkward questions would be asked so say nothing.

To make some kind of sense, given the undoubted dangers of cottaging and sex in the parks, as to why men took such risks, Houlbrook says, and I quote in full:

> Some men found it simply impossible to find privacy within the residential spaces they occupied. Those who were married or were unable to leave home because of poverty or youth could rarely bring a partner home. Even for those living independently in London's diverse residential neighbourhoods, privacy was by no means guaranteed. If they were not to remain isolated and lonely, such men had little alternative to seeking sex and sociability in the most dangerous public spaces.

Every week for two years Jeffrey J, a valet living with employers in Endell Street, met his partner in Hyde Park. This was not some casual pick up for a quick sexual encounter in the park. These two men were obviously devoted to each other but had nowhere else to go.

The key words here are: Isolation, loneliness, and sociability. Looking back to my own life prior to 1975, I remember how I longed to be able to drop my guard just for a few hours. To socialise with men like me in a relaxed, friendly atmosphere without any pretence.

Surrounded as I was by other human beings, I was still totally isolated and lonely for many years. So I can well understand why these men took such risks for the sake of some company with men who were just like themselves. Those of you who had the luxury of home, love, and companionship, perhaps shouldn't judge their behaviour too harshly. That sentence is not directed at you both personally, John and Bill, but rather to heterosexuals in general.

The cinemas and theatres in the capital were also places where gay men were able to meet and interact with relative safety during the 1920s and 1930s. The aisles stretching down on each side of the large cinemas were unlit and standing was allowed. This gave men a unique opportunity undercover of darkness to fondle and grope each other. Certain signals were employed by these men to tell others that they were available. Once the authorities cottoned on to what was going on lighting was hastily installed and standing was forbidden, this they said was for safety reasons. And it was at about this time that the usherette first appeared with her forever probing torch.

I didn't realize it at the time as I was far too young, but cinemas in the 1950s were still popular with men for the same reasons. Like most working-class kids, I often scrounged a couple of bob from my Mom to visit the local flea-pit, the Villa Cross cinema, and go to the afternoon matinee during the school holidays. Before I left the house she would always caution me to be careful and watch what I was up to, while telling me that if a 'strange man' came and sat next to me to just get up and move somewhere else. 'Yes Mom,' I'd say having not the first idea what she was talking about. Obviously my mother was very well aware of what could happen inside a darkened cinema to a young, unwary lad.

Just as in Wilde's day, the West End theatres such as the 'Alhambra' were a popular meeting place for gay men, where the various bars inside the theatre could be used as a discreet meeting place. Nearly all of the gay men using these places were of the well- dressed, middle-class type.

Up until now, I haven't mentioned the places where gay men were able to congregate in large numbers, not for sex, but to socialise. The large number of pubs, clubs and bars all over the West End provided a haven for the discreet gay man to meet other gay men. Being discreet though was essential as the 'normal' clientèle would quickly pick up and react violently to any outward manifestation of queer behaviour. This pub scene though seems to have been fluid and forever changing as the licensees of these pubs were likely to come under pressure from the police, once a large group of suspect men came to their attention. As no law was being broken, the police often used the 'keeping a disorderly house law', as a threat that they would have their licence removed if they didn't tighten up and control their customers. This was a serious threat to the landlords as without an LCC licence they'd be out of business. But it was also a dilemma for them as the gay customers bought in a great deal of money in beer and spirit sales. Most landlords were more than happy to have gay customers as long as things didn't get out of control and remained discreet, as they were a valuable source of income. One landlord in the 1930s angrily complained that after coming under pressure from the police and having to bar his gay regulars, his takings dropped by £100 a week, a huge amount of money.

Pubs like the York Minster, the Swiss, or the Marquis of Granby in Soho were all well known gay pubs in the 1930s, and you could often see a cross section of the gay world with men in evening dress mingling with and cruising workmen and sailors in a pub called the Running Horse. The upmarket night clubs were the preserve of the wealthy gay man though, the Hungry Horse and Chez Victor's in Wardour street were very popular in the 1950s, while the Trocadero, on the corner of Shaftesbury Avenue and Piccadilly circus was the most famous of all. It was exclusive, expensive, and for 'gentlemen only'.

There was one group of gay men though that didn't seem to be welcome anywhere, the outlandish and loud, painted queens who could be found all over the West End. Like men characterised by John Inmann in the TV comedy 'Are you been Served?', playing Mr Humphreys, or Melvin Haynes playing Gloria in 'It ain't 'arf hot Mum.' I had absolutely no idea until starting to research this article that so many flamboyant, and effeminate men existed in such large numbers in and around the West End. Wherever they congregated they immediately came under scrutiny from both the police, and the public. They were constantly harassed by the Met, forever being moved on, thrown out of pubs, and were both verbally and physically abused by the general public. They came in for such vitriol and hate and I admire them for their great courage in the face of terrible persecution. They refused to hide themselves away from the public gaze. This was one group of homosexuals who did truly experience persecution, but in the face of all of this they remained defiant, giving two fingers to an uncaring world. There's also a certain ambiguity in society's treatment of these men. On the one hand there was often a violent reaction towards them, but they could also find an amused tolerance and acceptance amongst the local population. But one thing is sure, they were true to themselves and had the courage of their own convictions no matter what was thrown at them. These men were all working class and had to earn their living the same as everyone else. During their working day they had to tone down their outlandish behaviour and dress more or less conventionally. They would, though, often embellish their attire by wearing garish, silk scarves or brooches. Large numbers of them seem to have worked in the hotel and catering industries, as waiters, kitchen help, and barmen. They could also be found, like Mr Humphries, in the large department stores in the capital. It's interesting that while there were a large number of these 'queens' as they were called, in London between the wars, by the 1960s, they'd largely disappeared off the scene. There are very good cultural and social reasons for this, which are very well and thoroughly explained by Matt Houlbrook in Queer London.

One of the most famous of all gay meeting places in London was the Lyons's Coventry street Corner House. This eating house was so popular that men would cue around the block just to get into the place. Opened in 1909, it became one of queer London's landmarks for four decades, and became so well known that it was talked about by gay men all around the world. Someone once described it as being like a 'giant garden party' and was used by men of all spectrums of the gay community. Men could eat, drink, and socialize while listening to the resident orchestra with no fear of the outside world.

I came across another set of places that had a thriving, underground gay life that during the many years of their existence seem to have never once come to the attention of the police, something that I find truly amazing. These were the bath houses that had come into existence in the mid-Victorian period and a few were still operating well into the 1960s. Two of the largest and most well known were the Savoy, and at the Imperial hotel in Russell square. They weren't of course gay, but as they were open all night with cubicles provided giving a large amount of privacy, they quickly became a regular meeting place for gay men, almost a social club. They were almost exclusively used by gay men during the hours of the night and during the whole of their history never once came to the attention of the police. One man, just after the first world war, said that he'd slept for a week in a Turkish bath, which meant that he'd barely slept at all. Both the Savoy and Imperial were large, elegant, and very reputable premises, and while the night-time attendants knew what was going on, as long as it was discreet, they turned a blind eye. These places weren't cheap though. A night in one of the better saunas cost about six shillings during the 1950s, quite a lot of money.

It's interesting that the 'gay sauna' enjoyed a huge revival in the 1970s and 1980s, and Martin and I knew many men who were forever rhapsodising about the latest sauna that they'd visited and which of them was the best. It has to be said, though, that these gay saunas were a hotbed of sexual activity where multiple sexual encounters during the course of one night were the norm. The gay bath houses of San Francisco were notorious for their nightly orgies and were largely blamed for the rapid spread of Aids in the USA during the 1980s. Sauna's are another thing that neither of us has ever had any interest in and as a result, many people thought that we were a bit weird.

One of the last places that I thought would be a safe place for men to go were the many reputable hotels that could be found all over the city. During the first half of the century, it was common, in fact an everyday occurrence, for two men to take a single room in a hotel for a night or two. This was to save money, and it wouldn't have occurred to the proprietors of these hotels to think anything of two men sharing a room. There are no recorded cases of anyone being prosecuted for 'gross indecency' inside a hotel room. The only time, and this was rare, when a hotel came to the attention of the police was when a young man went to them to make a complaint of sexual assault against a man that they'd been with. But as I say, this was extremely rare.

During the course of my research I came across mention of a place well known to the three of us, the old Union Jack club in Waterloo road. I stayed there for one night during the late 1960s while travelling back to Germany after a Christmas leave. The club was opened in 1907 to give servicemen a cheap lodging while on leave and to protect them from the temptations of vice. This, however, seems to have backfired as it was bang in the middle of a notorious red light-district. The presence of so many healthy young men attracted prostitutes and gay men like a magnet to iron filings. By the 1920s the UJ had gained a reputation as a place to meet gay men, and It was relatively easy to take someone up to your room after meeting them in Waterloo road or the West End. During the 1940s it became known as a safe place to *both* take partners and somewhere to *find* casual sexual encounters. In 1952, for example two men were caught together in a cubicle and the police were called. This kind of behaviour caused the authorities grave concern throughout the 1950s, and the place was put under surveillance by the military police. Despite this very few cases were ever detected and the Naval authorities were pleased that only 14 cases of indecency were reported between November 1951 and April 1953. The place became almost legendary. John Alcock, a regular visitor said the following:

> You went there because it was like Everard's bath house in New York – you just left your door open and somebody would come in and spend a couple of hours with you.

I've been surprised over and over again while doing this research at the huge number of incidents from Victorian times, right up to the 1950s, of the number of working- class men involved in homosexual behaviour. From the cavalrymen at Hyde Park Barracks, to the East End pubs, a great favourite with gay men, to young soldiers of the Brigade of Guards in the 1950s, and the comings and goings at the Union Jack club. Homosexuality and heterosexuality seemed to have become blurred and interchangeable. These young men were at ease in both camps (forgive the pun). They made no secret of it either, being totally open with their mates. In the East End for example, they would often discuss and joke amongst themselves about their various sexual adventures of the previous evening. Matt Houlbrook tells of a young Eastender, who one evening met a young girl in his local pub and later that night took her to bed. The next night he went back into the same pub, his local, said hello to the girl he'd been with the previous evening, and later was picked up by and had sex with a gay man. As I say, interchangeable. There are of course very good sexual, and social reasons for this phenomena which Houlbrook goes on to explain in great deal in his book. It's not within my remit to even attempt to explain what is in fact a very complex subject. I'll lend you both the book and you can read it for yourselves. I will just say this though, mainly because it fascinates me. Their masculinity was very important to them and they would not take a passive roll in any sexual encounter with another man. As this would make their behaviour feminine and threatening to their very real masculinity. As long as they were the dominant partner, their masculinity wasn't called into question and so they were happy. It also seems that once they married, these practices ceased and they settled down to domesticity and married life. As I say this is a hugely complex subject best left to Houlbrook, who is a far more expert than me to explain the many motives involved. I find the easiest way when talking about these young, working class men, is to think of their behaviour as being bisexual, although that's not necessarily accurate.

It does seem though, as if this behaviour had largely disappeared by the early 1960s. Houlbrook goes on to explain the factors involved in great detail. But he mentions a number of factors such as the huge rise in employment after the war when young men had more money in their pockets, the more readily intermingling of the sexes, and easily available contraception (something for the weekend, Sir?), where a young woman was more likely to have a sexual relationship with her boyfriend, to give you an idea. Given what I now know, I would say that it's interesting that all of my early sexual experiences were with other working-class boys and we didn't make a big deal out of it, but more of that later.

As I said very early on in this this letter, the working-class men who had these gay encounters during the first half of the century seem to have been willing participants, and viewed it all as a pleasurable way of making some extra cash. A man cannot fake sexual arousal, and as these men almost always took the dominant (male) role in these encounters had they not been willing, then they wouldn't have been able to fulfil their expected function. You can of course take a moral view point by saying that these young men wouldn't have had any sexual contact with another man had they not needed the money. That's possibly but not necessarily true, and you can't escape the fact that these young men, and all the evidence is there, truly enjoyed the experience. What I'm trying to say here is that the fact that they willingly took part in this sexual behaviour indicates to me that they had a great deal of the homosexual in their make- up. As I said earlier, perhaps the easiest way to describe them is as bisexual.

If you cast your own minds back to your late teens/early twenties, would you have considered having a homosexual encounter with another man no matter how much you were desperate for money? The answer has to be no. Why? Because homosexual behaviour would have been totally unnatural to you and not part of your make-up. I've often tried to explain this to straight men by saying that heterosexual sexual behaviour to me would be as unnatural as homosexual behaviour would be to them. I tell you now, that you cannot make someone gay: either they are, or they're not, as any gay man will confirm after making unwanted sexual advances towards a straight man. The reaction is very often violent. It seems to me that as far as human sexuality goes there are varying degrees and nothing is black or white. The truth is, it's a largely unfathomable subject. At least to a layman like me.

While writing this section a thought came to me about something Colonel Laurie, RAMC psychiatrist said to me at Millbank Military Hospital. He said that the sexuality of all males could be determined by using a scale going from one to eight. One being one hundred percent heterosexual, while eight indicated one hundred percent homosexual, and that most men were somewhere on that scale. This theory would perhaps go some way to explaining the behaviour of these young men. Although I have to say that I've never heard that point of view since.

After reading all of the previous pages on the behaviour of gay men in parks and cottages, etc. you could easily think that all homosexual men spent all of their time routing around London looking to have sex wherever they could find it. That would be inaccurate. In fact the majority of gay men avoided the cottages and cruising grounds of the parks like the plague. That's entirely understandable when the risks involved could mean arrest, prosecution, public disgrace and a life totally destroyed. Also, like me in fact, these men could find no pleasure in having anonymous sex in a public toilet or a park. The men who avoided outdoor sexual encounters became known as *respectable homosexuals* and they tried to make friends in a more social setting, often with great success. One of these 'respectable' gays, a lawyer, once said that if it meant going to a cottage for sex, then he'd rather go without sex at all. The thing that ruled the lives of these men was fear, something that I understand all too well. The ever present feeling deep inside the gut that at any time the mask could be torn off and that they would be discovered. It was explained in Houlbrook's book by a man called Antony Gray, who said:

> It's perhaps difficult for people ... to realize what the law meant for those of us that were 'respectable' and did care about the effects might be on our families ... by getting into legal trouble ... the disgrace involved was absolutely unthinkable.

A book was published in 1953 by a writer called Rodney Garland, called 'The Heart in Exile'. Although a novel, the author was intimately involved and familiar with every aspect of the London gay scene. Using the word 'underground' to describe gay(s) he sums up this majority group of gay men by saying the following:

> The majority of the underground do not go to queer pubs, clubs or even parties, do not linger round public lavatories, railway stations or other recognised or obvious places. There are thousands of young inverts among the millions of normal young men who live with their friends in boarding houses, small flats, hostels, clubs, associations, some times under the roof of ... parents ... secrecy is complete and scandals are rare. The underground is everywhere.

This idea of the 'respectable homosexual' came into focus in the 1920s, and was to cause a schism between the newly emerging 'gay liberation movements' that flourished after 1967. Again, more later.

In 1935, two men in their mid-forties were caught having sex in the back of a taxi in a back street in the West End. They were duly arrested, and bailed to appear for trial at the local magistrates court. This was not a case of a pick up for casual sex, as the two men had been together in a loving relationship for a number of years. To them, the thought of a trial and public exposure was too much to bare and they decided on suicide. The night before there appearance in court, they climbed up onto one of the London bridges and leapt together into the Thames. The next morning, the prosecuting council asked where the two defendants were. He was told of the previous nights suicide attempt, and informed that one of the men had drowned, while the other had been rescued and was recovering in hospital.

George V is reputed to have said after hearing of a homosexual incident, 'Oh, I though that men like that shot themselves.'

> I do not think that I am far wrong when I maintain that at least half of the suicides of young men are due to this one circumstance. Even in cases where no merciless blackmailer persecutes for urning, but a connection has existed which lasted satisfactorily on both sides, still in these cases even discovery, or dread of discovery, leads only too often to suicide. (John Addington Symonds, c1895)

Sources:

Queer London by Matt Houlbrook
Prince Eddy and the Homosexual Underworld by Theo Aronson
The Secret Life of Oscar Wilde by Neil McKenna
The Heart in Exile by Rodney Garland
The Dilly Boys by Mervyn Harris

6
And Where Does David
Fit into the Picture?

Well, Bill, and John, that brings an end to my brief, gay history. I hope that you've both found it illuminating and of some interest. It's time now to turn our attention to my story, and as it's my story, I can tell it with a great deal of authority.

> The stigma attached to homosexuals may be unfair or
> exaggerated, but it exists and induces in the homosexual
> feelings of shame, inferiority and social alienation.

Those words were used by Mervyn Harris in his book, 'The Dilly Boys'. That sentence gives an accurate description of the way many gay men felt about themselves, and I was no exception.

As you both know, I'm from a working-class background and was born in Birmingham in 1948. While hardly luxurious, the house that I grew up in was a vast improvement on the the back-to-backs that had been my mother's childhood home. Her father had been killed during the Great War, and she and her younger brother, Walter, had been largely raised by her grandparents. Times were very hard for them, but they didn't experience the extreme poverty of many of their neighbours and seemed to have been well cared for. My mother though, was to suffer great heartache in her early years, and although she was too young to remember her father, she and her brother were brought up to revere her father's memory. Her mother, Amelia, seems to have been absent for large parts of her childhood. She was to die in tragic circumstances of a back street abortion in 1927. What made it even more tragic was the fact that mom, aged only fourteen, came home from school one afternoon and discovered her poor mother lying in a pool of blood close to death. She died that night in hospital. This event was to have a profound affect on my mother for the rest of her life.

My Dad's family background couldn't have been more different. The Spencer family had been basket makers for generations and had originally come from Dudley. They were a large family having five children that I knew as a child, and I believe there were two others who'd died at a relatively young age. By the early 1900s William Spencer was a successful man and while not wealthy, the family were comfortably well off, and could be described as middle-class. They were also cultured and music played a great role in all of their lives, while the children were all encouraged to play musical instruments. William himself was a talented violin player and my dad, John, learned to play both piano and 'cello. Sunday evenings were often spent around the piano playing together as a family. I suppose that's where I get my musical ability from.

136 Church Street in the Birmingham district of Lozells was made up of quite large houses. Built in the 1880s for blue-collar workers, they had three upstairs bedrooms with an attic above, while the ground floor consisted of a font room, usually only used on family occasions, a middle room used for family living and the only one warmed by a coal fire in the winter, and a large kitchen with a scullery attached. Each house had a long narrow garden with an outside toilet. There was of course no bathroom or central heating. My upbringing was unremarkable and much the same as most of the other kids in the neighbourhood. Mum and dad made sure that we were well clothed and had good nourishing food. We were a typical working-class family, dad going out to work, while mum stayed at home and cared for the children. There were four of us, with quite an age gap between

us. Mum often remarked that she thought that there was too big a gap. The war had disrupted normal life so much with mum being evacuated to North Wales with my older brother, John, during the Birmingham Blitz of 1940. My grandfather, William Spencer, was killed by a German bomb at his home in Aston in October 1940. My father went to a temporary morgue in the city to identify the body and saw, lying next to his father, the body of a young women cradling her dead baby in her arms. Dad went straight home, told mum to pack some things, and she left the city that day. When she came back in about 1942, my older sister was conceived with me following in 1948. My youngest sister wasn't to come along until 1958. Money must have been tight but dad was typical of his class and would not allow mum to go out and find a job, something that I expect she longed to do. To him, it was his job to bring in the wages, and for her to be the home maker, the traditional housewife. And it was mum who was the disciplinarian of the family, and who taught the children good manners and good behaviour. And on the rare occasions that a slap was required, and it was rare, it mum who usually did the slapping.

The streets were our playground with an absence of any parental control, unlike today. In the school holidays we'd wander far and wide getting into all kind of scrapes and only going home when our bellies started to rumble. In short, I was a normal, scruffy kid and not much different from any of the other boys and girls of the neighbourhood. My dad was very unusual in that he had no interest in going to any of the many local pubs for a pint or two in the evening, and this was unusual. He always said that he just never liked the taste and so left it alone. I suspect much to the relief of mum who'd seen too much drunkenness during her own childhood.

Dad always made sure that we had a holiday each year at the seaside, almost always staying in a typical English boarding house. I remember those times with great affection sixty years later, from waiting for the taxi to arrive to take us to Snow Hill station, to clambering aboard the carriages pulled by the huge black steam engine; the grey smoke and steam spiralling up towards the soot stained glass roof of the station. Our days were spent making sand castles on the beach and paddling in the sea, with promise of an ice cream if you were very good. It was just a typical working- class holiday of the 1950s, with 'kiss me quick' hats, candy floss and donkey rides, a time now long past.

One year, by way of a change, dad booked us a holiday at Bolton Abbey in Yorkshire. The first week was to be in a converted railway carriage, while the second was in a converted railway station. The railway carriage was parked by the side of a branch line that was still operational, no health and safety in those days, and was fully operational with a station master, and a young porter. In my mind, I have for many years used this holiday to pinpoint my sexual awareness. I was far too young to understand my feelings, being barely nine years old, maybe even younger, but I remember that there was something, a feeling of excitement bordering on adoration. And the object of this affection? The porter at the station was only about sixteen years old, with blond curly hair and a wide, winning smile. And I fell instantly in love with him. An innocent love of course, as I didn't know anything of the feelings that occur between human beings that lead to a sexual relationship. From the moment that I woke up in the morning till the moment that I went to bed at night, he was constantly in my mind and I followed him around like a lovesick puppy. The poor lad was very tolerant of me and allowed me to trail behind him as he went about his duties. I vividly remember spending a blissful, sunny afternoon sitting on an embankment at the side of the railway line, while he was stripped to the waist; his muscular torso gleaming in the sunlight, swinging a pickaxe up and over his head bringing it crashing down on the ballast by the line. On the day that we left to move on to our second week at the converted station I remember feeling a deep sadness. Do you know, Bill and John, I can still see that young lad in my mind as if it were yesterday. Right or wrong, I don't really care, it's those few days spent in Yorkshire that in my mind showed me my future sexuality.

Unusually for a boy of my age I devoured the Sunday newspapers. My dad took the two working-class staples, *The News of the World* and *The People*. I remember that both of these newspapers in the mid-fifties devoted acres of print on the evils of homosexuality, reporting with relish and in great deal every sordid little detail that they good dig up. Journalists scoured the capital investigating every aspect of the 'Evils of Homosexuality'. A journalist, Douglas Warth of the *Sunday Pictorial*, traversed London's queer spaces in order to expose '*an unnatural sexual vice which is getting a dangerous grip on this country.*' The *News of the World* continued in this vein saying in an editorial, '*The grip of this form of vice is tightening. Only the searchlight of public opinion will reveal the extent of this evil at our midst.*'

During the war with the threat of death ever present, morals came crashing down and for many gay men, with the availability of willing partners to be found amongst the members of the allied forces, and the useful cover of darkness given by the blackout, it was almost a 'utopia.' A sentiment that I've heard many times from men who'd lived through it. The clampdown that came after the war took a different direction from anything that had come before. The emphasis was now to be on the 'predatory gay, the corrupter of youth and the enemy of traditional family life'. In truth the government were scared. There was more money and jobs around and young people were beginning to challenge their 'olders and betters', something that had never been seen before. Society was changing and standards were being lowered; this was regarded by those in high places as a grave danger to the British way of life. So the 'queer' was regarded as a ' *predatory and lustful danger to the nation and its manhood , which embodied a wider crisis of post war Britishness.'*

Houlbrook in 'Queer London', sums it up thus:

> The encounters between urban queer culture and the law ensured that public knowledge of 'Homosexuality' was framed by an overarching narrative of sexual danger. If that danger was located in different qualities and influences, these were all, nonetheless, underpinned by a common assumption: the queer threatened British society. Indeed that threat was so pronounced as to warrant extremes of public vitriol, and what were nominally draconian forms of regulation.

Note the term, 'extremes of public vitriol'. He continues:

> The operations of the law, in this schema, were imag- ined as protecting the national community against what was variously as a 'Disease,' a 'Plague,' a 'Canker', and a, 'Foreign invasion'.

Good Lord Almighty, I never realised that we 'queers' wielded so much power and that we were such a 'grave threat' to the fabric of the nation; I wish!

Reading all of this in the early twenty-first century you can hardly credit that people genuinely believed all of this hogwash, and dare I say it again, is it not the kind of language perpetrated by the men in 'black' against another minority in Germany. And yet this is exactly the kind of society that I grew up in, in the 1950s. People genuinely believed that 'queers' were 'sick perverts' and 'deserved everything that they got'. As a growing child, my subconscious mind absorbed all of this negative and hateful comment. I read it in the newspapers, and saw it all around me in the attitudes of my parent's generation, and the boys and girls that I was growing up with. Is it any wonder then, that I, as one of those 'dirty little queers', should start to feel fear and self-loathing, and try to hide my feelings in case I was somehow caught out, and my filthy little secret was exposed for all the world to see? These negative and destructive feelings were to haunt me for many years into the future.

In 1959, I, along with 80% of my fellow schoolchildren, failed the dreaded eleven plus examination and was sent off to Birchfield Road Secondary Modern school for boys. Gower Street would have been much nearer but it had such a bad reputation that mum decided that Birchfield was the better option. It was at this time, while my male friends started to look at the female sex with growing sexual desire as their raging hormones started to kick in, that my eyes turned very much towards them. As my hormones were as powerful as theirs, it's little wonder that I viewed them in exactly the same way as they were starting to view the girls. By the time that I was fourteen, very much like certain boys at the English public schools, I'd already had a number of sexual encounters with some of the boys in my class. While some of these experiences never amounted to more than an adolescent grope, some went a bit deeper. There were two boys in particular who I met with on a regular basis. Graham was one, and as his mother and father both went out to work and with his house empty, we went there often after school. Another boy was called Doug. His parents on a Saturday night, went off to the local working-man's club, giving us an ideal opportunity to get together for a couple of hours. I must have got a bit of a reputation though, as one day, two boys in my class approached me and invited me back to their place after school. I declined simply because they lived in an opposite direction to me making my journey home too far.

We shouldn't read too much into the behaviour of these boys. The word 'phase' is often used to explain this type of sexual experimentation in adolescent boys and it usually vanishes as they mature. To them, it was a pleasurable way to get some kind of sexual relief, and was better than the more obvious method. They knew that as they got older there would be plenty of opportunity to meet a member of the opposite sex and start courting, but in the meantime...

I remember one evening with Doug, when he turned to me and said, very seriously, 'That's the last time, Dave, it's been great, but I've got a girlfriend now'. He smiled and shrugged his shoulders as if to say, 'No more'. This was just a couple of months before we left school and we parted as good friends. Strangely enough though, at that time, I don't think that any of us felt any kind of guilt, and that does include me. My guilt was to develop shortly afterwards when I realized deep in my heart, that my feelings towards my own sex were never going to go away and that my 'phase' would last for the rest of my life. I guarantee that everyone of those boys did indeed meet the woman of their dreams and went on to marry and raise a family.

I left school in 1963 able to read and write but not much else. You both know my story well and so there's no need to repeat it here except to say the following. For many years I've pondered the question to just why I joined the army. I've often said to you both, that the reason was that I didn't fancy working in a factory and wanted something better, but is that strictly true? Certainly that seems to be my conscious reason, but what of my subconscious. Something that I've never mentioned to you before is that for many years I practised self-hypnosis. I understand the power of the subconscious more than most, and believe me it's very powerful indeed. The question that I've very often asked myself is was I trying to run away, to escape and hide. It's a question that's unanswerable and hardly matters now. But I do often wonder.

Arriving at the Brigade depot, Sutton Coldfield, came as a huge shock, not just to me, but to everyone of the other boys. Once we got used to our new circumstances though, and as we grew in stature and confidence, we quickly adapted to our new environment and started to relish it. None of us had ever been away from home before we'd always been treated as children, but things were now very different. For the first time in our lives, we had to stand on our own two feet and put our boyhoods behind us as no one was going to hold our hands. Given that we were only fifteen years old and in many ways still boys, we matured more quickly than our counterparts on the outside in 'civvie street'.

Friendships quickly developed and it was at that time, that I had my first serious gay relationship. I think that it's true to say that gay men have an instinct about someone and try to get close to that person to test the waters. Remember that you had to act with great caution as your instinct could be totally wrong, which could easily lead to your being branded 'a queer', the last thing that you wanted. It was at this time that I well remember my excitement, thickly laced with fear. Ray and I liked each other obviously, but circled each other trying to see what the other was thinking. One evening after tea, Ray, who was learning flute and went on to serve in the Northumberland Fusiliers band, came up to me and quietly told me that he was going down to the library and would I like to join him. The message was clear, and I quickly agreed. Ray told me to meet him at the library later so that we wouldn't be seen going down there together. I was quickly to learn that this kind of secrecy was essential in the homosexual world in those days. Never, ever, draw attention to yourself, and always keep in the shadows. Is it any wonder that we quickly adapted to living in some kind of murky underworld, and that we lived our lives in fear of discovery.

Ray would always go to the guardroom to sign for the key, and I would join him later. I don't remember anyone ever coming into the library while we were there during those evenings. Most of the lads were in the TV room, or playing billiards in the NAAFI, and weren't at all interested in visiting the library. We always made sure that the lights were turned on and that we were clearly visible from the outside. We sat facing one another with our heads stuck in a book, for all the world like a couple of keen, junior 'bookworm' soldiers. How quickly we learned to hide in the shadows in those days, never being able to drop our guard and living a perpetual lie. After about an hour, Ray would take the keys and go and lock the outside door while I turned of the lights. We'd then go into the windowless toilets, and the rest I'll leave to your imagination. We often did exactly the same thing in the band practice room. Ray would sign for the key and it would be much the same as the library. We almost got caught out once, when someone loudly rattled the outside door one evening, and we quickly readjusted our dress. Ray unlocked the door and one of the boys came marching in. He glanced over at me but said nothing, saying that he wanted the record player as the one that they'd been using was 'on the blink'. What he though I don't know, but nothing was ever said about it as far as I know. These regular encounters with Ray were to continue for most of our boy service. And while these meetings were undoubtedly exciting, they were also laced with a great deal of guilt. We were after all a couple of queers and were products of our time and our society so therefore felt self-loathing at our behaviour. I certainly regard those two years as being my awakening to my true sexual orientation. It was at this time, aged barely sixteen, that this all pervasive fear seeped into my core, undermining my self-confidence and virtually destroying my self-esteem. Over the following years, this was to take a huge toll on my health, and It would have made no difference to me had I been inside, or outside the army, the result would have been the same.

I only ever saw Ray once after we left boy service, a brief meeting at Bassingbourne. There is however an interesting postscript to this story. Very recently, I was able to get in touch with him again after almost fifty years. I knew that he'd served twenty-two years and reached the rank of S/SGT. He married his first wife, but this ended in divorce when it was discovered that she was having an affair with another member of the band. He later married again and had a daughter. Sadly, his second wife died of cancer, and he left the army in about 1985. Now this is the interesting point. It seems that the first thing that he did after leaving the army was to go straight back into the gay world, a world that he claims to dislike, but nonetheless still frequents today. He lived for six years and had a relationship with a man, before they parted, and he now cares for an elderly gay chap in Bournemouth. I have to ask myself, did he marry in the first place to give himself some cover. And was his marriage a smokescreen to mask his real sexuality. Did he live a lie for all of those years? I suppose that he did, but find it sad that he felt unable to be open about his real identity. I've known many men like Ray over the years and often rage at a society, which because of its attitudes, forced men to spend their whole lives deceiving those who loved them.

By the time I left boy service in 1965 I was a competent clarinet player and so my musical future was secure. Not bad when you consider that I'd never played a clarinet, or any other musical instrument in my life prior to my enlistment, but within two years I was able to find my way around the instrument, and was always to play on the first clarinet stand. My first posting was to Hamlin, but this was to be short-lived as the regiment returned to the UK after my first six months. Our next posting was to be Watchet, a place that I grew to love in many ways. The first thing that I discovered on joining the band was that there was a culture of drinking, sometimes heavily, throughout the band. This was made very easy as the band had its own club which was run by the band members and was closed to outsiders. If you have the keys to the sweetshop, then you're likely to be tempted to eat all of the sweets. As there was virtually no control over the opening and closing hours of the club, especially at the weekends, then heavy drinking could go on until the early hours of the morning. In Berlin for instance, I've known the band club to open on a Friday evening and virtually stay open until the early hours of Sunday morning. Actually, this rather suited me as it gave me some camouflage. I didn't stand out from the crowd as being a heavy drinker as everyone else seemed to be, too. What I mean by this is that I'd started to rely on alcohol to support me in my constant inner turmoil. I felt totally alone and isolated, this was a huge problem for gay men of my generation, but was compounded for me because being in the army; I had no chance of meeting other gay men like myself. The nagging distress always present deep inside my stomach eating away like a canker never subsided, except when I'd got a few drinks inside me and I could look at the world through a haze of booze. You mustn't think, though, that we all walked around semi-drunk twenty-four hours a day, we couldn't have functioned as a band had that been the case. And as you both well know, any bandsman who couldn't do his job would quickly find himself in a platoon carrying a rifle. I put it down to the endless stamina of youth. And in the whole of my army service I never once fell foul of the authorities because of drink. I tell you now though, I felt an awful lot more confident with some alcohol floating around my system. I used drink as a coping mechanism against a hostile world. I don't know how widespread heavy drinking was within the line bands back then, but I suspect that it was common, as very many bands had their own clubs.

I've often been asked why I didn't quietly slip away into the gay world at weekends and leaves. That is to underestimate my fear, the fear of discovery, the fear of being picked up by the police in some kind of a raid and found to be a member of the armed forces. After 1967 it became much easier for gay men to socialise and meet other gay men.

The pubs that gays frequented became much more open and didn't any longer come under police surveillance, but I didn't know that at the time, and I'd still have been to frightened to take the risk. Not only that, of course, but I wouldn't have known where to go or where the gay pubs and clubs were. Plus the fact that I was still very much in 'denial' about myself. No, I was on my own. But I'm sure that very many homosexual servicemen did just that and disappeared into the London gay scene, and had I had someone in the know to hold my hand and show me these places, then I would probably have gone along with it. But with a great deal of trepidation on my part. To be honest, and with the benefit of hindsight, it would have been the most sensible thing to do. Not only would I not have been so isolated, but, to be frank, I would have been able to relieve my longing for sexual contact with another human being. It didn't happen that way though, so there's little point in dwelling on what might have been. I was very fortunate that I became a very popular member of the band and was generally well liked. On the surface I was a happy cheerful lad who mixed well with the other lads. They had know idea of the underlying unhappiness that was constantly there. Out of necessity I became very adept at hiding my true nature and putting on a happy cheerful front.

But life went on. As I made clear in my last book I had a wonderful time playing all kinds of music up and down the country as a member of the band. I can't emphasise enough that unhappiness of those years were hidden deep within myself.

During the three plus years we were stationed in Watchet I did have the odd sexual encounter. These were always brief, unsatisfactory, poisoned and tainted by guilt. Two of them were with members of the band believe it or not. I'm sure that you remember the story I told you about Norman? He was the chap who beat me up while drunk one night. He'd been celebrating his twenty-first birthday, which gives you an idea of how young we still were. I tried to help him out if you remember by backtracking while giving evidence against him, something that was to cost me dear. It was Norman who later turned against another member of the band called, John, while we were stationed in Berlin. And if you remember the whole band turned against him that time and he was forced to transfer to another band. So what do John and I have in common, and why did Norman turn against us in that way, It's very simple. Both John and I had sex with Norman, at different times I hasten to add, and it was this that made him turn against us. Norman was one of these men who hate themselves for being 'queer', and turn this self loathing against other 'queers'.

Another encounter that took place with another band member rather makes me smile even after all these years. There was an E-flat clarinet player in the band called Tony. I've mentioned the word 'instinct' to you before, and Tony, who was one hundred percent gay, quickly sussed me out. The trouble was, I didn't like him, and certainly didn't have any sexual interest in him, but he wore me down and in the end I gave in. This was the night, believe it or not, before the band's KH inspection. We found somewhere quiet and private and, well you can guess. The next morning I was sitting in front of 'Jiggs' Jaeger playing the overture to 'Iolanthe' if only he'd known.

Shortly after this encounter the police turned up and arrested Tony. I still don't know if they were CID or SIB, but he was marched away and we never saw him again. I have no idea as to why he was arrested, but did hear that it was something that he was involved in while on the KH pupil's course. I believe that pornography was involved in some way.

For the next few years nothing changed for me; how could it? I functioned as a person and continued to do my job, drank far too much and didn't eat enough. I had the odd sexual encounter, but with always the same result, unsatisfactory, guilt-ridden, and meaningless. By the time 1967 and the partial decriminalisation of homosexuality came, something that I was both aware of and envious of, I had to face the fact that my life could never change while I was still in the army. The trouble was, that by the time of our departure to Berlin, I still had at least six years service left to do and no way of getting out.

Berlin was by far the best posting that I ever had, and many happy hours were spent soaking up the music of the Berlin Philharmonic, which gave me a great deal of comfort. I was fortunate enough to share a two man room with an old pal of mine from boy service days, Roy Corbishley. He'd known about me since boy service, but neither of us ever spoke of it.

This would be a good place to ask the question, what did the other band members know about my sexuality? I realize now, of course, that they certainly knew that I was gay, they had to have done. They were intelligent men, and no matter how much I tried to hide the truth from them, the mask must have slipped from time to time, in fact I know that it did. But I still kidded myself that my guilty secret was well hidden and safe. I suppose that this was a psychological safety mechanism. I'm sure that had I thought that they knew, I would have undoubtedly spiralled out of control with possibly tragic consequences. Burying my head in the sand and denying the truth was the only option that I had open to me. I was helped greatly by this as not one of those men ever made any derogatory comment to me: not ever, and for that I will take my gratitude to the grave. I suppose that I was very fortunate in being so popular and well liked. This may be difficult for you to understand, Bill and John, how could you, having never been through anything like it yourselves. The truth is that by the time we returned from Berlin in 1971, I was in despair and couldn't see any way out of my predicament. There were times when I cursed my nature and asked why me, why couldn't I just be 'normal' like everyone else, but that was something that I knew that I could never be. The realisation that if I was in civvie street, I could now lead my life as I wanted to was a burden. Once the stigma of criminalisation had been lifted, I would have been more than happy at anything public opinion could throw at me, in fact I would have relished it. That was the key you see, de-criminalisation. But for me it might as well never have happened as homosexuality was to remain illegal within the armed forces for very many years into the future.

Catterick, God how I loathed that place. After a two week leave we laid eyes on our new home for the first time. My morale plummeted as I looked around the 1950s- built accommodation. Eight bloody men to a room, it was back to boy service again. No privacy, something that I longed for, no peace and quiet with the 'Black Dyke Mills Band' in competition with radio one or 'Coronation Street'. There and then, I decided that I was going to do something about it, either that, or go mad.

Saturday in the local town, Richmond, was market day and so the pubs were open from morning till night, something that we took great advantage of. A group of us would congregate in a pub near to the market square, while the gamblers amongst us studied the racing form for the Catterick races that afternoon. I sat there, morosely sipping a pint and my eye happened to fall onto a copy of the local newspaper. An idea came into my head and I quickly turned to the 'accommodation for rent' section. Going down the columns my eye fell on an ad for a small studio apartment for rent. When I saw the address, I realized that it was in a building that we all knew well. The ground floor was occupied by a popular café used by the many tourists and hikers that came to the area during the summer months. We used it a lot and could often be found after a session in the pub devouring large quantities of sausage, egg and chips.

The rest of the large building was used as a B&B, with two studios up in the attic. Jean, the owner and a lovely woman, also lived on the premises. Jean, incidentally, became a good friend to me over the coming months. I quickly finished my pint, leaving the lads with their heads planted firmly in the paper, and headed over to the café. I asked the waitress if Jean was about and was sent up to the first floor where I found Jean sitting up in a large double bed with a shawl over shoulders and a fag hanging from the corner of her mouth. Of course, she knew me well and invited me to sit down. I explained why I was there and she suggested that I take a look at the place on the following Monday evening. A young squaddie lived there with his heavily pregnant wife, and he was to be given a married quarter. I said that I would and made her promise not to let go to anyone else. Heading back to the pub I felt a great deal of excitement, mixed with a certain amount of apprehension. Back then, it was unheard of for a single man to live off barracks. I wondered would they give me permission and if not, would I go ahead and do it anyway?

As it turned out, I needn't have worried. On the Monday I looked the place over. It wasn't much, consisting of one large room with a double bed in the corner, an electric hob on a large table, and two armchairs, with a bathroom just off the main room. Not much maybe, but to me luxury. Before I even got permission I told Jean to hold it for me and rushed back to barracks. The next morning I knocked on Rod Parker's door and with my heart in my mouth, told him what I wanted. Parker had taken over the band from Fred Fitch while we were in Berlin. I have to give him his due, he was far more forward looking and modern in his outlook and as he was only a few years older than me, I think that he had some sympathy at my undoubted unhappiness as far as our accommodation went. He said that he'd see what he could do and promised to get back to me. He gave me my answer within a day or two and it was positive. I would not, however, be able to claim back any of my barrack room or food charges, not that that made any difference to me in fact, I'd have paid them.

I was to spend some very happy hours in that studio, the peace, tranquillity and privacy were beyond price. I went to my 'local' most evenings and got to know the locals well. I was eating better than I'd eaten for months and drinking a bit less. I'd usually pop in to the 'chippie', which was just next door to my place, for a fish and chip supper, and then sleep like a baby. Of course nothing changed as far as my inner feelings went, and I often wish now, that I'd bitten the bullet and spent some time exploring the gay scene in Darlington or York, but I still didn't have enough courage. In fact, had I done that, I would probably have saved myself a lot of trouble, trouble that almost brought me to the attention of the police. By this time I was into my early twenties and the mask was starting to slip.

After Berlin, I became more and more distant from the band. I don't mean that I no longer got on so well with the other band members, as to them I was just the same old Dave, but I couldn't relate to them any more. I wanted to be with my own kind, with people that understood me and my feelings, people that I could be my real self with, which was something that I could never do with the other band members. There was also another change that took place in the band after Berlin. We had a new intake of ex-junior bandsmen arrive from Bassingbourne, and these kids were far more savvy than I'd ever been at their age. I admit that I was starting to become predatory, and some of them viewed me with suspicion. Not that I was stupid enough to give them any cause for complaint but I spent too much time hanging around with them, and they, suspecting an ulterior motive, were wary around me.

I was rapidly promoted at this time too, quickly going from lance corporal to full corporal far more rapidly than was normal. I think that I know the reason for that now. The second Fusiliers band were next in line to send a full corporal to Bassingbourne as an instructor and I think that Rod Parker had me in mind. Although still two years in the future, he seems to have been planning ahead.

As Christmas of 1972 approached we started to prepare for our first tour of Northern Ireland. A great step into the unknown. My time in Belfast with the band is well documented as you know, so I don't need to go into detail here although there are one or two incidents worth mentioning here. We were due to leave Catterick early one morning for Liverpool to catch the very ferry and so the night before I headed for my local to drown my sorrows. I remember that it was quiet in the bar and I started to chat to a young, and very attractive apprentice jockey, who trained with one of the local riding stables. We hit it off and after a few beers I invited him to my place, an invitation that he was more than happy to accept. Of course, we ended up in bed together, and after he left at about 4 am I started to get ready to make the trip to Ireland with a heavy heart.

There's one incident in Belfast of a sexual nature that's important. There was a lad in the band called Alan and I'd been chatting him up for a long time. As I said earlier, my mask by this time what starting to slip and I was becoming far less cautious. Although nothing had ever happened between us I could tell that he was curious On Christmas eve we'd spent the evening in the NAFFI bar in Palace Barracks, our Belfast home at the time. Three para. were the permanent battalion. Officially we were only allowed two cans of beer a night, but you could always find ways around that and we got pretty much plastered. Walking back to our hut, Alan suggested that we go into the washroom block which was totally separate and quite a way from our accommodation. I quickly accepted and we went into one of the bathrooms and locked the door. We spent sometime in there and quietly left to return to the band's accommodation. On

Christmas day we were off duty and the army had laid on a traditional Christmas dinner served by the officers and senior ranks. One of these men, a C/Sergeant, and the battalions MT officer, approached me and asked if I was Spencer? I said yes, and he quietly told me to follow him, which, with a sense of apprehension I did. We went over to a quiet corner and he turned towards me and slipped my army ID card into my hand. As I looked down at it I felt a deep nausea which threatened to upend my dinner onto the floor. He was very discreet and said, 'this was found on the floor in one of the bathrooms this morning.' He looked at me intensely and I detected a good deal of sympathy in his gaze as he continued, 'I suggest that you're far more careful in future as someone else might not be so understanding.' I murmured my thanks as he nodded his head and turned away. Who found the card I've no idea and why it was handed to him is another mystery. The reason that I'm telling this story is because some months later, a member of the band told me that this particular senior rank was gay. He knew because they'd at one time had a discreet affair. Since then I've read various articles on this subject and it seems that the army were prepared to turn a blind eye, as long as the soldier involved was discreet about it and if it in no way brought the regiment into disrepute. I read an article written by an army general at the time of decriminalisation of homosexuality in the armed forces in 2000. He said that two of the bravest men that he'd ever served with were homosexual.

Over recent years I've given this whole subject of homosexuality in the army some serious thought, a lot of it borne out by my recent research for this letter. If you think about it logically and simply in terms of statistics, given the size of the army in the 1960s/70s, then a percentage of those men then serving would have been gay. But given the very real dangers involved in any sexual activity would have been hidden deep underground, but I'm sure that it was there. We should remember that two years in Wormwood Scrubs for the civilian was bad enough, but that would have meant at least two years in Colchester Military Prison for the serviceman which I would argue, was far worse. When you look at the number of sexual encounters that I had within my own immediate circle and within a band of only about thirty-five, it does raise some interesting questions. Most of the people that I had that kind of contact with went on to live 'normal married lives'. I suppose that it just shows again that human sexuality is a very complex subject and reinforces what I've said previously.

I was very lucky again during that Christmas and it wouldn't be the last time that fate smiled on me over the coming two years. Keeping the façade in place was becoming ever more difficult and I was starting to take dangerous risks.

Not long after our return from Belfast in early 1973, I was called into Rod Parker's office. He asked me if I'd go down to Bassingbourne that September on a two year posting as an instructor, I immediately and without any hesitation said yes. I can still remember how I felt at his offer. I could see a way out of my increasing unhappiness with the way my life was going in the Fusilier band, and this gave me the perfect opportunity. As I said earlier, I felt detached from them and no longer a part of the band. I put this down to my increasing feeling of isolation and my desperate need to make some kind of changes in my life, and this could perhaps be the answer. Although I can't for the life of me see what meaningful changes I could really have made. Perhaps I was just grasping at straws. I've often wondered if Parker had some kind of ulterior motive in making the offer, but perhaps I'm being overly paranoid. Had talk about me filtered up to him and did he see me as a potential problem that he wanted to get rid of? The question is unanswerable now, but anyway at the time I was happy to go.

My morale lifted over the next few months and I continued to be happy in my little studio. My own little world. There were two more important events that occurred during those final months and need to be retold here. I found one of the ex-boys from Bassingbourne, a young lad called Doug, incredibly attractive and it was more than lust on my part as I had a genuine affection for him. He is the only person whom I ever had a relationship with in the army that I really had deep feelings for, and had things been different, well, who knows? I've used the word 'instinct' a few time during the course of this letter to you both, and I had this strong intuition about Doug. The way that we glanced at each other sent out a powerful message. Doug was tall, slim, and boyish with light brown hair and blue eyes. To me he seemed unhappy, and I wondered if we both shared the same unhappiness, and for the same reasons. It was he who broke the ice one day as we sat talking quietly together. He started to tell me about a sergeant who was an instructor at Bassingbourne and who was known to us both. He was due to return to the band later that year and Doug told me that, although married, he'd been playing around with one of the junior bandsmen. Although Doug didn't admit it to me, I suspect that that junior bandsman had been Doug himself. The relationship had been consensual on both sides. I cautioned Doug to keep all of this to himself and not to talk of it to other band members about it. This sergeant was very popular and Doug could have made himself a lot of enemies, especially as he couldn't, or wouldn't, substantiate the allegations. Better, I said, to say nothing. When I got home that night I realized that Doug had given me a very clear signal and that the ball was now very much in my court. After all, why tell this story to me in particular?

The opportunity presented itself not long afterwards. Rod Parker had decided that he'd like to make a record of the band and a temporary studio was set up in a gym in one of the Catterick barracks. He employed a sound engineer and scheduled a Saturday to do the recording. He announced that once we'd finished for the day, we could have the Sunday and Monday off. We were having a smoke break and I walked over to Doug and asked if he'd like to come over to my place that night and stay over. He immediately agreed and we arranged to meet in a local pub. I suggested that he keep our arrangement to himself. He smiled and said, 'Of course, I'll tell everyone that I'm going to Darlington'. With my heart beating at the prospect I walked away quietly satisfied. We met up that night and had a few beers before heading off to my studio. As I said earlier, my feelings towards him were deep and warm and unlike anything that I'd ever experienced before. I suppose that's why that night is so vivid all of these years later.

But of course, it all went sour. The next morning, I got up leaving Doug in bed. I quickly got dressed and made the excuse that I was going to buy the Sunday papers. As usual, I felt guilty about the whole business and wanted a bit of time to thing things through. I bought the papers and slowly walked back to the front door of the house. When I put my hand in my pocket to take out the keys, I realized that I'd left them upstairs and that I was locked out. There was no bell to my studio, and as it was early in the morning, there was no one around to let me in. It took me a good hour to attract the attention of Jean's son who was still in bed. He came down, and was not best pleased at being disturbed. He let me in and I walked upstairs to be confronted by Doug who, by this time dressed, turned on me for walking out like that and leaving him wondering where I was. I tried to convince him that I'd left my keys by mistake, but he was very angry, and I don't blame him. After all, we'd spent the night making love and instead of lying in bed together talking, having a cigarette and drinking a coffee, as you would expect from two people who'd spent the night in shared sexual pleasure, I'd got up, got dressed and walked out. Rob left just afterwards and I believe, took himself off to Darlington. I could have cried at my crassness and unfeeling stupidity, but the damage had been done and was irreparable. Doug must have felt used by me and reasoned that after I'd had my way with him, was no longer interested and wanted to see the back of him. I've carried a great sadness about with me for over forty years for that incident. Because I really believe that Doug and I could have had a deep and loving relationship had it not been for my unforgivable behaviour on that Sunday morning.

Since writing this, and completely out of the blue, I've just heard from Doug. He's now fifty-nine and lives in Southampton. Doug like me is gay and has led his life as a gay man, but sadly, his experiences have largely been unhappy which is a great shame. At last, and after almost forty years, I've been able to lay the ghost to rest, and apologise for my behaviour towards him on that Sunday morning all of those years ago. We intend to keep in touch.

I was to have one more encounter before I left for Bassingbourne, and it nearly landed me in front of the police. My local was just a few minutes walk away from the studio and was a bit more upmarket and avoided by squaddies. I could be found in the lounge bar on most nights and got to be well known by the locals. There was a woman who came in there regularly and I got to know her well. We spent a lot of time socialising and I think that she genuinely liked me. I walked in there one Saturday night and sitting with her was a young man of about eighteen. He was incredibly good-looking and of course, I was immediately drawn to him, which was foolish of me to say the least. He was in the sixth form of a local grammar school and hoped to go on to university. Over the coming weeks and months I saw a lot of him and his mother and on one Saturday night, she invited me back to their house after closing time. By this time I'd had a bit too much to drink and I was very quick to accept the offer.

Once there I was very reluctant to leave and overstayed my welcome. I remember that his mother after dropping numerous hints excused herself saying that she was off to bed. After she'd left, and by this time the worse for wear I started to chat him up, fortunately for me it was no more than that. As the reception that I received was cold, I quickly got the message, made my excuses, and left. Unknown to me, his mother had been standing behind the door listening to every word that I'd said.

When I got back from the barracks on the Monday evening, one of the girls who worked in the café told me that Jean wanted to see me urgently. My heart fell as I had an idea what this could all be about. Jean and the boy's mother were lifelong friends, having been at school together, and as soon as I walked into her room she turned on me with fury. Calling me all of the names under the sun, she asked me just what I'd been up to on the previous Saturday and without giving me chance to reply told me that the boy's mother had been to see her that afternoon. As I said earlier Jean was a good friend to me and I think, had guessed my sexuality from the outset. She told me what a complete fool I'd been and didn't I know that you should never s*** on your own doorstep! After a while she calmed down, and told me that she'd dissuaded her friend from going to the police which is what she fully intended to do. Her tone softened as I mumbled an apology. She looked sympathetically at me and advised that if I was looking for that kind of sexual experience then I should take myself off to Darlington or a large city where I was unknown.

I had a very close shave over that incident and was very lucky to get off so lightly. I was starting to skate on very thin ice by this time, and as I got older, having been forced into involuntary celibacy having nowhere to go to meet other gay men, I was playing a very dangerous game. Had I been sober that night it would never have happened, but booze has a very nasty habit of stripping away your natural inhibitions with sometimes dreadful consequences. I never set foot inside that pub again and fortunately, left Richmond not long afterwards to go to Bassingbourne.

If you think about my situation it's understandable that my sexual frustration should start to show itself. I was in my early twenties, and many of my contemporaries were by this time married, and those that weren't had a satisfactory sex life. While I had nothing. As I've said many times before, had I been able to mix with gay men like myself, none of these problems would have shown themselves because I would have been able to satisfy my sexual needs. But fear held me back, something that I now deeply regret, but that's hindsight.

Before I was due to go to Bassingbourne in September, the band were to do a six week tour of the Midlands which I should have taken part in, but fate was to step in with a vengeance.

The band went on two weeks summer leave and I headed down to my aunt's in Worthing. Aunt Fan, as we called her, was my dad's elder sister, and live alone in a small flat. She never married, and had moved to be near her sister, who promptly up and left to join her son in Canada leaving Fan alone and isolated. She was by this time in her late seventies, and was very glad of my company. While I was there, I started to feel very ill indeed. Constantly in pain and vomiting, I went to see Fan's GP who must have been at least seventy-five and he gave me a sick note for a week. I'd been in the army for long enough to know the rules about sickness for a soldier on leave. I should have reported myself to the nearest military unit as being sick and handed myself over to them. I was so ill, that I foolishly ignored all of the rules and travelled back to Catterick having been technically AWOL for a week. The journey back was a complete nightmare for me and the next morning, I headed straight over to see the MO. As I walked in, he took one look at me, told me that I was as yellow as a dog, and phoned for an ambulance to take me straight to Catterick military hospital. I was immediately put into isolation as I was highly infectious, and diagnosed with infected hepatitis. This upset Rod Parker's apple cart, as he was now his first clarinet player short, and so the band had to leave without me.

I had a lovely few weeks in that hospital. I spent my days reading endless books and lazing around being waited on hand and foot. I went before a medical board and was medically downgraded for two years, and after a few more days leave, I went back to the empty band lines, packed an MFO box, and headed to Bassingbourne and my final couple of years in the army. Although I didn't know that at the time. Incidentally, many years later and just before I was due to have an operation in Luxembourg, the doctor informed me that I'd never had hepatitis. It's obvious to me now that the liver damage had been caused by my years of very heavy drinking, and given that I was only twenty-three that gives an indication of how much I'd put away over the preceding years.

There's just one amusing post-script to this story. While still in hospital I was informed by the medical corps RSM, that I was to charged with being AWOL for a week. With a big grin on his face he told me that an ambulance would take me to the barracks the next morning, wait for me, and drive me back afterwards. Not long after the RSM's visit my doctor came to see me, winked, and told me to tell the CSM that I was still highly infectious and to keep his distance. I did just that and was gently marched in to the OC, far more gently than was normal, and was admonished for not abiding by the rules. End of story.

David as a child aged about 5
in the back garden, Church Street

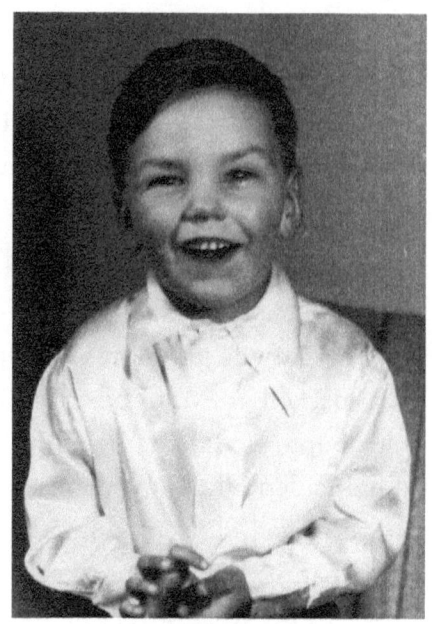

Taken at the time of the
Queen's Coronation, 1953

David as a child aged about 5
in the back garden, Church Street

Taken at the time of the
Queen's Coronation, 1953

The wedding of John Spencer, about 1964.
David, aged 16, wearing the uniform of a
junior bandsman in the Royal
Warwickshire fusiliers

A lovely, early photograph of Martin,
aged about 4

Martin, aged about 10, on holiday at St Anne's-on-Sea with his father, mother, and aunt Ede

Martin with his mother and father while a pupil at grammar school, aged about 14

Martin in the back garden of the Jackson family home, again aged about 14

Martin, aged about 10, on holiday at St Anne's-on-Sea with his father, mother, and aunt Ede

The earliest photograph of David and Martin taken together in 1977. The photograph was taken at the well known and popular Birmingham gay club, The Grosvenor

Two photographs (above and top right) of 10 Ampton Road, Edgbaston, our much loved first home together in 1976. Photograph taken on a revisit in 2011

A studio-type photograph taken in the early 1980s while on holiday in Bournemouth

On the same holiday

Martin and David, Toronto, Canada, 1983

Martin

Martin at a friend's in the Dutch town of
's-Hertogenbosch, mid-1980s

Photo taken in Luxembourg
at about the same time

Martin on holiday in Burgundy,
France, 2003

David and Martin, about 1984

Christmas day, Luxembourg, late 1980s

Martin on holiday in
Burgundy, France,
2003

On the same holiday

The two of us,
Belgium, about 2004

*Christmas day,
Lucerne, Switzerland,
2004*

*David, just before a
concert with the
Luxembourg
Philharmonia
Orchestra, late 1980s*

*The Jackson and
Spencer families at a
party held in Worcester
in 2005. Millie
Spencer and Beatrice
Jackson in foreground.*

At the wedding of Martin's niece, Diane, summer 2009

David and Martin on holiday, Aston Cantlow, Warwickshire, 2005

David laying a wreath on behalf of the Royal British Legion at the war memorial, Broadway, on the one hundredth anniversary of the outbreak of the Great War, 4 August 2014

David in the garden at Kingsdale Court, Broadway. Note the medals worn on the right: the DCM & MM of CSM Stephen Jackson, Martin's grandfather, and the three Great War medals awarded to Rifleman Walter Smith, David's grandfather. Both men were killed in 1917.

At the memorial, 4 August 2014

David, about 2003

7

Bassingbourne, and a
False Sense of Well-Being

When I arrived at the Queen's Division Depot I quickly lost sight of my real problem: I was still a homosexual in the army and nothing could change that. I loved Bassingbourne. I loved my job, and my boys thought the world of me. I cut down on my drinking and for the first time in years, had a good opinion of my-self. My self- esteem soared and I started to enjoy music again, I came back to life. I was smart and well turned out, and looked every inch the instructor. My sexuality ceased to be my every waking thought and I managed to push it into the back of my mind. Which goes a long way to explain what I did next.

One morning after I'd marched the boys over to the education centre, I headed over to the Director of Music's office. Captain Don Price was a nice man, and I liked him a lot, a man that I could do business with. My army service was due to come to an end in 1975. I could have left while still serving at Bassingbourne and done something different with my life, something more compatible with my lifestyle, but I didn't. Like I say, my new found confidence and enjoyment blinded me to the reality of my situation. I knocked on his door, went in, and saluted. He told me to take a seat and asked what he could do for me. I'd thought it all through the previous evening and proceeded to tell him what I had in mind. I said that my time was due to run out the next year and this is what I proposed. He listened carefully, as I went on to explain my plan. I said that I'd be prepared to sign on for a further three years, on the condition that I be allowed to spend a further two years as an instructor at the depot. That would have meant that I'd serve four out of the five years at Bassingbourne leaving me just one year back with my band and anyway, I figured that a lot could happen in the next four years so who knows where I might have ended up. The other thing that was uppermost in my mind was the prospect of a third stripe, a very real possibility if I played my cards right. Price was enthusiastic at the idea, as it would save him having to search for someone to replace me at the end of my two years. The instructor's posts were very unpopular generally as no one wanted to be away from their band for two years and possibly lose a chance of promotion. I couldn't have cared less if I never set eyes on the Fusiliers band again, and so my idea had a great appeal to the D of M. And so it was agreed, I'd sign on for three more years and spend four of the five years of my remaning army service in Bassingbourne, which is what I did. With the benefit of hindsight it was a foolish thing to do. I was so fulfilled with my life at the depot that I lost sight of the real problem. I suppressed it and buried my head in the sand.

I did of course have my own room, but lived in the same accommodation as the boys and there wasn't an evening when one or two of them would pop in for a chat or to tell me about their latest girl-friend. Don't think though, that I allowed them to be too familiar, there was a line that they couldn't cross and they knew it. If they got too cheeky, I'd say something like, 'You'll be calling me Dave next.' It was truly amazing at how much more mature these boys seemed when compared to boys of my boy service days. They were very wise to the ways of the world and couldn't be treated as we'd been in the early sixties. I employed one of them to do my kit every night, but made sure that he was paid and I never took advantage of my position, something that they respected. We also had some awesome brass players, most of them with a brass band background, who'd been playing since early childhood. I conducted a brilliant brass quartet and they were more than capable of rattling through the overture to 'Euryanthe' by Weber. I did a lot of conducting in those days and gave clarinet lessons at the local comprehensive once a week. It's little wonder then, that with my happy musical life, and general well being that I was able to put my problems to one side. I was surrounded by extremely attractive young men, but I never once had any inappropriate thoughts about them. My happy existence carried on in this way for over a year and I remember that I hadn't felt so good about myself for many years.

It couldn't last of course. I couldn't change my nature and didn't feel able, because of my fears, to take myself off to London, which was just down the road, in search of what I wanted and needed. I now realize that this is what most gay servicemen did in those days. They just merged into the nearest gay scene and became invisible, but that again is hindsight.

Because I was the only single member of staff, it usually fell to me to take parties of boys on various trips away from Bassingbourne. The married men didn't want to be away from home for days at a time, and I was more than happy to go with the kids for a few days out. It was on one of these trips that I was to meet my nemesis.

8

Nemesis

Nemesis has caught me in her net: to struggle is foolish.
Why is that one runs to one's ruin? Why has destruc-
tion such a fascination? Why, when one stands on a
pinnacle, must one throw oneself down? No one
knows,but things are so.

Oscar Wilde

The definition of nemesis in the English dictionary is as follows: 'A
goddess usually portrayed as the agent of divine punishment for
wrongdoing or presumption (hubris)'. My nemesis came in the form
of a cocky and extremely attractive young man called Chris. I don't
remember taking much notice of him before, he was just one of the
boys and he'd never spent any time, as far as I can remember, in
hanging around me; at least no more than most of the others. Chris
was an Essex boy, very sure of himself, and was the type that usually
got what he wanted. At the same time he was boyishly charming, the
type that you could forgive for just about anything. In fact, every gay
man's dream. I first became really aware of him on one of these trips
away. He was on the tennis team, and I'd taken them to take part in
an army, junior tournament in Colchester. Chris was coming to the
end of his boy service and was due to join his band at the end of the
term. When we arrived and were shown to our accommodation, I
was told that because of a shortage of bunks I'd have to use the same
barrack room as the boys. Of course, I had no objection and walked

over to a double bed space which was slightly separated from the rest of the barrack room. When I walked in, who should be standing there but Chris with a smile on his face. Had we not had a junior NCO with us I'd have been more than happy to let him stay where he was. But I was aware that as the bed space was a bit more superior and private than the others, then I should give it to Junior L/Cpl North, as a bit of a privilege, which is what I did. As Chris left, he gave me a look, which had I have been a bit more 'savvy' would have set alarm bells ringing in my head. The temptation of Adam comes to mind. Whenever I think of him after all of these years, it's just like the boys of the East End, as described by me earlier in this letter, self confident and with no sexual hang-ups whatsoever.

I could go on in this vein for pages, but just let it be said that Chris, who I now realize had had very many gay sexual encounters over the years, probably from an early age. He was very experienced sexually, far far more then me. None of this can in any way excuse me from what was to happen in the near future though. I have no intention of going into any detail here, in fact, most of that night is a complete blank to me, something that I can go some way to explaining later. In a nutshell, Chris and I went to bed to together one night back in Bassingbourne. I do remember that his obvious sexual experience far surpassed my own but not much else.

When we lived in Luxembourg in the early 80s, I went to see a very fine psychiatrist called Jules Molitor. Molitor had studied at one of the finest psychiatric hospitals in the world in Chicago. It was a pleasure for me to know him for many years and he put my life under a microscope. Jules knew as much about me as I knew about myself, and he became a good friend to me and Martin. I have to tell you that when I first told him of my treatment by the army after my sexuality came to light, he was horrified at what he saw as the barbaric treatment meted out to me at Bassingbourne. He couldn't believe that a civilized nation could treat any one in the way that I'd been treated there. He was appalled that an army psychiatrist, Lt/Col Laurie, should have given me some tablets and sent me on my way. I must say that Jules Molitor had a point, given that I was so vulnerable, he should have made sure that I was somewhere safe, and not in a position to harm myself as could easily been the case. He was, after all supposed to be a doctor and should have seen my mental state, especially as by this time, I'd started to drink heavily again. To be told that 'Nobody likes a drunk' hardly seemed adequate. Remember that at that time I hadn't been charged with any crime, and although I didn't know it, never would be. But anyway that's beside the point.

Jules and I discussed in great detail the night that I'd spent with Chris and the events leading up to it. I'm sure that you've both heard of 'alcoholic amnesia', where a person has no memory of what they've done the night before because of a large intake of booze? This blackout with Chris is very similar and medically it's called 'Dissociative Amnesia'. It's very common amongst people who've suffered sexual abuse, or other such trauma, where the conscious mind blocks out the whole experience. There's also another similar condition called 'Psychogenic Amnesia'. This is caused by very high levels of stress and depression. I'm not going to try to blind you with psycho-babble, but it does give you an indication to my state of mind for the days and weeks after my encounter with Chris; and goes a long way to explain my lack of awareness as to exactly what happened that night. It's important to remember that no one ever knew what had happened between myself and Chris. Obviously, had it come to light, I'd have been facing a few years in Colchester followed by a dishonourable discharge. I could have easily shrugged my shoulders and carried on as if nothing had ever happened. Chris wasn't going to say anything about it to anyone else that's for sure. So why didn't

I shrug my shoulders and walk away? Did I feel that I'd betrayed my trust and had too easily allowed myself to be seduced instead of walking away. Well yes, partly, but it went a lot deeper than that. I remember sitting in my bunk just after this incident with Chris and taking a long, hard look at my life. For years I'd ignored the obvious; I was in the wrong job. Living in an army society where my behaviour was still regarded as criminal, I was very aware that outside in civvie street that was no longer the case. Far better to be sweeping the streets and being able to lead my life in the way that was right for me, I reasoned, than forever looking over my shoulder and being racked with guilt because of my sexuality. I had to go, no matter what it cost me. And after this latest incident with Chris, which was only one of many, remember the boy in Richmond, I knew that it was only a matter of time before I found myself in real trouble if I stayed in the army.

Given my state of mind after my night with Chris, I was barely able to function, and deeply unhappy, I just didn't know what to do. In fact, I should have been inside a hospital. To this day, I can't say with any certainty that what I did next was a conscious or subconscious decision, and like my night with Chris, is almost a complete blank. There was a young recruit doing his basic infantry training at the depot before being posted to his band. He was a clarinet player and I was keeping my eye on him. One evening I walked into the band practice room while he was practising. In an act of almost suicidal stupidity, I came on to him. I chatted him up, but was careful not to approach too closely and made sure that I didn't lay a finger on him. I talked about this with Jules Molitor many years later and it was probably a subconscious need to end my misery, no matter what the cost. I do remember the look of shock on that lad's face as I turned and left the room. The next morning, I reported sick. I told the MO that I was suffering abdominal pain. Given my recent medical history, he decided to put me into the camp hospital for a few days of observation. I sat in my room and waited for the axe to fall as surely it would. I didn't have long to wait. That evening, John Millgate, the BSM came into my room and with an icy tone asked me for the keys to my bunk and lockers. I remember well his look as without another word he walked out. John and I had always got on well, but as I'd known all along, once people knew that you were a 'queer', then you instantly became friendless. Things happened quickly after that. I was discharged from the hospital and told to report to the guardroom where two members of the SIB were waiting to interview me. One was a C/Sergeant and the other a Sergeant, I remember. I was told that a complaint had been made against me and that I was under investigation. Again, I don't remember much of that interview, my mind has just blocked it all out. I didn't deny that I'd chatted the boy up, short of calling him a liar, how could I? But I was careful not to admit to anything else to these two men, who I saw as a grave threat to me. I was told that I could leave and would remain under investigation pending further charges been brought against me.

My next visit was to the CO. This was the man who told me that if he could, then he was going to crucify me, and believe me, John and Bill, he meant it. He was another who only a few days previously had returned my salute with a cheery good morning. Of course I wasn't let anywhere near the boys, and was given a job pushing paper clips around an office in the HQ block. I lived in an empty block with a room of my own and might just as well have been inside a prison. I was totally isolated. I also got a message to report to the adjutant, a captain in the Royal Anglian Regiment. As I entered his office, I noticed a black briefcase that I recognised as belonging to me sitting by the side of his desk. My heart skipped a beat, as he pointed at it and asked where the keys were. I was quickly getting used to thinking on my feet, and while the key was sitting in my pocket on my key ring, I unhesitatingly told him that I'd left it at my aunt's in Worthing. He wasn't unfriendly and nodded telling me to get it as soon as possible so that he could take a look inside. I said that I would, saluted and left. So what was in the briefcase? I'll tell you. At some point in the previous months I'd bought an American gay magazine. By today's standards it was not pornographic, more erotic, but would have been damning had the SIB got hold of it.

My next port of call was Millbank Military Hospital and my meeting with Laurie. He said two things to me during that interview. One was that I was sexually immature. That was something that I had to agree with. Given my situation since the age of fifteen it's hardly surprising. The second thing that he said I knew was just plain wrong. He told me that he didn't think that I was homosexual. 'Bull****', I thought to myself, but didn't say so. I'd quickly started to view anyone wearing an army uniform as my enemy, and I clammed up and gave absolutely nothing away. I wasn't going to make it easy for them. Don't you think it odd that I should distrust even an army doctor? But I trusted no one and over the past few weeks had toughened up, thinking if you bastards are going to treat me like a criminal, then I'll start thinking like one. Laurie told me that he was going to recommend my discharge from the army, and with a huge inner sigh of relief, I thanked him and left, clutching a bottle of some kind of powerful anti-depressant. I now have my army medical records, obtained by me through army records. I have a copy of the note given by Laurie recommending my discharge. However, he says that this is only to be granted if no 'criminal evidence' could be found against me. It's a good job that I didn't know that at the time. I returned to Bassingbourne that day with a feeling of optimism, I could see a glimmer of light at the end of the tunnel. Little did I know that getting to the end of that tunnel was going to take a good few months. I remember that the adjutant asked me how I'd got on and the look of surprise that crossed his face when I told him that Laurie was going to recommend discharge.

Meanwhile, the SIB were busy beavering away in the background doing their best to find something, anything, that they could dig up as evidence against me. They'd thoroughly searched my personal belongings, but were unable, no doubt much to their frustration, been able to find anything. They travelled far and wide interviewing anyone who they thought could help them in their quest for evidence, even going to KH to talk to one of my old boys who I'd been close to. Ian was a nice lad from my own regiment and we had been close, and while I suspect that he did know about me, nothing had ever happened between us. When you think about it, the SIB were on a hiding to nothing. No one was going to admit to them that they'd any kind of sexual relationship with me as they themselves, would be admitting to a serious sexual offence. In the end, they came up with a big fat zero! Of course, I knew nothing of this at the time. And as I thought that I might still have to spend a few months in Colchester, I prepared my self to the ordeal of having to tell my parents. I asked for permission to go home for a weekend leave which was granted.

On the journey up from London, I did everything that I could to get smashed, all to know avail. It seemed that the more I drank, the more sober I became. Perhaps I was getting harder and angrier for the predicament that I found myself in and needed a clear head. That night is etched on my memory and will be with me until the day I die. My dad, a working-class chap and well into his sixties by that time, listened as I opened up to him while the whole story came flooding out. After I'd finished, he looked at me, and said very quietly, 'Dave, I don't care what you are, you're my son'.

I went back to Bassingbourne on the following Sunday now ready to face whatever was to come. In the end, nothing came. There was not a shred of evidence against me, at least nothing that would stand up in a court of law. When it came down to it, it was nothing more than my talking to a soldier, and that was hardly a criminal offence. They knew absolutely nothing of any sexual encounters that I'd had during my time in the army and in the end, had to admit defeat. The weeks and months that followed were a nightmare for me. I now knew what it had been like for previous generations of gay men who were exposed to public gaze and vilified because of their sexuality, because they were 'queer'. I hid myself away, rarely leaving my room, and only then at night. I'd sneak around to the back entrance of the NAFFI, where a sympathetic manager would sell me some cans of beer and a couple of sandwiches; Jews and the Nazis always comes to my mind whenever I think of this time, yet again. Probably the cruellest thing ever to have happened to me in my life was at Bassingbourne. The corporals' mess were having a dinner night, and I had no choice but to attend. I was ignored by my fellow band instructors, and shunned by the other NCOs, as I sat, head down, picking at my food. It was what happened afterwards that to this day, makes me boil with anger. As entertainment, the mess had laid on a stripper, and they somehow made sure that I was sitting right at the front. This big-breasted young woman, no doubt directed by the corporals, made straight for me, shoving her breasts directly into my face, to howls of laughter from my 'fellow NCOs'. Just after that, I walked out followed by the sniggers of these men. They didn't know it of course, but they did me a favour that night. Incandescent with rage at my treatment, I was determined to start demanding answers as to just what was going to happen to me, it had gone on for long enough. That rage has stayed with me for all of my life, and right from the start after leaving the army, it was God help anybody that tried to humiliate me because of my sexuality: never again. There were individual acts of kindness towards me at this time though. The RSM was as kind to me as he could be given the circumstances, and I'll never forget a newly promoted, young sergeant from the Queen's Regiment, who came over to me and sympathised at my predicament. With my new found determination, that morning I walked into the office of my then boss, and asked if I could talk to him.

He, too, was facing the end of his career but for very different reasons from my own. A major, he'd been injured in an accident and walked with limp. I got on well with him and he seemed to view my situation with some sympathy, always treating me with courtesy. I knocked on his door and asked if I could talk to him. He nodded and told me to come in and close the door, sensing that I had something important to say. I didn't waste any time as I said that I found my position intolerable, and that I felt that I was purposely being kept in limbo. I continued by saying that if I were to be charged with any crime, then surely the SIB would have charged me by now. I pointed out to him that I'd been interviewed over four months previously and not heard a word. Not only that, it had been almost the same amount of time since Lt/Colonel Laurie had told me that he'd recommend discharge. I admitted that I was at the end of my tether and didn't know how long I could continue this twilight existence. He listened to me carefully and when I'd finished, he nodded and just told me to leave it to him. I thanked him, saluted, and left. My office was just next to his and I was able to hear every word of the conversation that followed. He phoned the adjutant and asked him what the hell was happening to Corporal Spencer's discharge papers. This confirmed to me that there would be no charges laid against me and he knew it. I heard him say that this had gone on for long enough, and that it was beginning to look as if someone was purposely dragging their feet. After a while, I heard the major tell him to get his finger out and do something about it. Two days later, my discharge papers came through. Things happened fast after that, and I remember handing in my kit, and doing the rounds of the various departments for administrative reasons. On the morning that I was due to leave I walked into the adjutant's office and politely asked if I could take my briefcase. He looked at me, and said, 'I never did get to see what was inside that case, did I?' 'No, you didn't,' I replied before giving him a little smile. I picked up the case and left without another word.

Before I leave this chapter of my life behind for good, I'd like to share a story with you. A couple of weeks before I left, I was standing outside my accommodation block. A squad of young soldiers appeared being marched along by a young , junior NCO. By the time that I realized who it was, it was to late for me to move and so I stood my ground. The NCO and squad were all my old boys and were being marched to the education centre. Yorkie, as he was known, saw me and as they approached he gave the order, eyes left, to a man they whipped their eyes over to the left and I was able to look into their faces as they marched past. In all of the years since then I've never forgotten that moment. It seems that those boys still had some affection for me and were sad at my misfortune. Shortly afterwards, I was able to talk quietly to a junior bandsman that I saw one evening coming from the NAFFI. He told me that the young recruit who 'informed' (his words) on me was getting hell from everyone for his betrayal. I got no pleasure from that, as the poor kid had just been in the wrong place at the wrong time.

9
Post 1975, and a Whole New World

Now well into old age, I view my life as being pre-1975 and post-1975. The day that I left Bassingbourne marked the end of what had been a difficult period in my life, and I was determined that from now on, I intended never again to be anything other than honest with myself and lead my life in a way that was right for me. That day in the summer of 1975 was my 1967 moment. Homosexuality was no longer a criminal offence in Britain, something that was of crucial importance to me. I didn't give a damn about society's attitudes towards homosexuality, just as long as I didn't have the stigma of criminality hanging over me. Perhaps you can now better understand my lifelong anger towards the state and their vindictive law that had criminalised generations of men just like myself. Sitting on the train heading towards the Midlands that day I wasn't jumping for joy or dancing in the aisles, but I did have an overwhelming feeling of contentment, and a quiet happiness, and I didn't immediately head towards the nearest gay bar in Birmingham. Rather, I went home and tried to get my life into some kind of stability and order.

The first thing that I needed was a job. Actually, I was no more qualified than I had been on the day that I'd joined the army twelve years previously. The Birmingham Symphony Orchestra weren't going to fall over themselves to give me a job, and I hadn't got a clue what I was going to do. That's another thing that I mark as a changing point in my life though; 1975 was the year that things starting going my way in all aspects of my life. There were lots of jobs on offer in the security industry run by companies like Group Four, and as I couldn't even put up wallpaper or paint a windowsill, then I didn't have a lot of choice. The security companies were always on the lookout for ex-servicemen and I had no problem being taken on. It didn't take me long to figure out though that as these companies paid peanuts, they usually got monkeys. The hours were long, minimum wage, and not at all rewarding, but as I had no choice, I shrugged my shoulders and got on with it. I can remember, though, how happy I felt during those weeks and months that remained in 1975. I felt so free, and was no longer continually looking over my shoulder. For a few months I was doing night shifts at Birmingham airport. It was just like doing a guard duty in the army and just as boring. But then things took a turn for the better when one day I received a telephone call from my Group Four boss. He told me that they needed someone to work days at the Prudential Building Society offices in central Birmingham, and was I interested. I immediately said yes as it was a day job and at least I'd get a good nights sleep. I enjoyed the few months that I worked at the Prudential. Sitting at the reception desk I was able to meet a lot of people and quickly became well known by the various people who worked in the large buildings offices. I quickly came to the notice of the boss of the Pru', mainly because I took my security job seriously. It was only two years earlier that Birmingham had been rocked by the pub bombings and everyone was conscious of the threats. There was a great bonus too. The Prudential employed a large number of attractive young men and I made a point of getting to know them. There's one who particularly sticks in my mind even after all of these years. We became friendly, and he invited me to spend the weekend with him when his mother and father were away, but this was not as it seemed. It had obviously not crossed his mind that I was gay, and when he realized that I had more in mind than a night at the pub he quickly backtracked and came up with some excuse. The only reason that

I'm telling this story is highlight the way that I'd changed in less than a year. I was no longer denying my sexual preferences, and while I wasn't wearing a 'Glad to be Gay' badge, like many gay men at that time were, I didn't make a great secret of it either. The young man's reaction was interesting too. There was absolutely no hostility from him it was simply a case of, thanks, but no thanks, and we continued to be good friends. This gives an indication of the way people, especially young people, were starting to view homosexuality in the mid-1970s. It also made me realize that it was time that I started exploring the vibrant Birmingham gay scene. This was a bit difficult at the time though, as I was still living with my parents in Redditch and had no transport.

I quickly noticed a number of smartly dressed men came into the Prudential every afternoon. They all wore grey suits, and went up to the offices of Customs and Excise on the first floor. Once I got talking to them I found out that they were all employed by the Bank of England, which was situated just across the churchyard a short walk away. Many of them were ex-servicemen either army, or Royal Navy, and one that I recognised, Bob, had been a corporal in my own regiment. I became very friendly with an ex-naval man called Jim, and I've often said that he and I shared some kind of a psychic link. Jim came in one day and headed over towards me. He told me that their was a vacancy coming up on the security team and that I should apply as I was just the type that they were looking for. He urged me to phone a Mr Hoblyn straight away and handed me his number. I've often wondered since then if I would have even bothered if he hadn't been so insistent. As he wasn't going to take no for an answer I lifted the receiver and dialled.

Hoblyn answered the phone and I told him who I was and why I was calling. To my great surprise, he invited me to send in my CV, which is what I did the next day by handing it over to Jim. I was phoned a couple of days later and invited for an interview on the Friday morning. Of course, I was delighted but had a niggling worry eating away at the back of my mind. I'd sent my army 'Red Book', and as you probably both know, this book is given to all servicemen when they leave the forces. The red book gives a full record of a man's military service. I had no worries about my written reference which had been done by my friend the major with the gammy leg. In fact it couldn't have been better had I written it myself. It described my service as being 'Exemplary' and went on to paint a glowing picture of my army service, which I believe was only the truth. What worried me, though, was what was written on the following page where it gave my reason for discharge as being 'Services No Longer Required'. It's always angered me that this vindictive labelling of servicemen who'd left the forces on the grounds of their sexuality should have happened. When anyone reading the service no longer required comment they were bound to ask for an explanation. It had the whiff of something being 'not quite right' about it and left a stain that you would carry around for the whole of your working life. It was either a case of never showing it to a potential employer or if you did, risking some uncomfortable questions. Given that my reference was so good, I was very reluctant not to show it, but realized that I needed to come up with a satisfactory explanation. Fortunately, neither Hoblyn or the other man at the interview knew anything about the armed forces so I came up with an explanation that I hoped would satisfy them. After thinking about it, I decided to go on the offensive as soon as I walked into the room, which is what I did.

I pre-empted them once I'd sat down by saying that I supposed they'd seen the services no longer required label. They replied that they had and wondered what it meant. I then proceeded to mix fact with fiction. While I'd been with the band I'd suffered a hernia which had been caused when I was marching up a hill playing, 'The

Standard of St George' march. This was at some carnival or other during a summer tour. It was unpleasant to say the least and I'd been admitted to a military hospital for an operation while I was at Bassingbourne. This was carried out successfully and I returned back to the depot and carried on as normal. All of that was true. I then started to fictionalise my story. I told them that because this could happen again if I continued to play, I was given a choice by the army either to transfer to another branch of the service, or accept a discharge under 'services no loner required' which is what I'd done. They both nodded and seemed satisfied by my explanation, going on to say how good my reference was. There followed a few more questions and then they both thanked me and said that I'd hear from them in due course. Walking back to the Prudential I was mildly satisfied and argued that I'd done the best that I could given the circumstances.

A few weeks passed and every time one of the bank men walked in, I'd raise my eyes only to be given a shake of the head. By this time all of them knew who I was and were all routing for me. One morning one of them came in and handed me a letter and with a wildly beating heart, I opened it. I was invited to attend a medical with the banks doctor. I straight away phoned my dad and told him about the letter, as he, being in the working world knew all about these things. Without any hesitation he told me that I'd got the job, as that's the last thing that any company did prior to offering a position. He was of course right, and a few weeks after my medical I was given a letter telling me that I'd been accepted and was asked to start on a given date. At last, things were really starting to go my way and after years of being unhappy with my life, I felt a real sense of optimism and joy. It makes me smile now but in the weeks that followed before starting at the bank, and each time that I walked past on the way to the Prudential in the morning, I'd be whistling a march well known to the three of us, 'Hollyrood'. You should understand that getting a job with the Bank of England was quite something as it was a very prestigious and world famous organisation. I felt a great sense of pride at working there and felt that I'd achieved something worthwhile against all the odds. Although things were slowly beginning to change within British society, it would have been an act of madness to admit my sexuality at that interview. Believe me, at that time the Bank of England lay at the heart of the 'Establishment', and had I given the true reason for leaving the army, then I'd still be sitting at the Prudential today.

It's unnecessary to go into what the job entailed here in great detail. Needless to say the bank's security was phenomenal and our control room, where we spent a large amount of time, was bomb-proof and with a huge bank of monitors covering all of the vital areas of the bank. We had a direct line to police HQ and throughout the night they would be contacted and a password would be given. This was changed every twelve hours. During the mid-1970s there was something like five hundred million pounds in the treasury, as the vaults were called at the bank. God knows what that would be today. Our other main function was to prepare the orders of cash for the clearing banks to collect. The main banks, Lloyds, Barclays, etc. had their own security vans, and access to the collection area was controlled by us. We never took money to any of the banks as that was their responsibility. On the days that we had a delivery of new notes from London, which arrived by train and was delivered on two container lorries, the whole of the city centre went into lock down, and was escorted from the station by police cars, flashing blue lights, and outriders. All of the police were armed. Orders for collection by the banks often totalled hundreds of thousands of pounds in various denominations in the course of the day. We were surrounded by vast amounts of cash and it's little wonder that we just viewed it as being so much paper. We were very well paid, and I was ridiculously proud of my Bank of England account and distinguished, grey cheque book, which always raised an eye whenever I presented a cheque. Interest-free mortgages were also part of the package, meaning that we could afford to buy houses that were out of reach of most house buyers. The bank certainly looked after, and well rewarded, its staff. We did of course work nights, with three night shifts followed by four free days, giving us plenty of free time. I often had to pinch myself as I looked a my good fortune at having such a job. I felt myself very lucky.

On the day that I started work at the bank I couldn't have known that life still had a number of pleasant surprises in-store for me. During the few weeks that followed my acceptance at the bank, I started to look around for a place of my own in Birmingham. I had no problem finding a small studio that was very similar to my Richmond bolt-hole. I quickly moved in and was very happy there, but I still had a problem. I was woefully ill informed about the Birmingham 'gay scene', and was itching to start experiencing a gay life style without fear. This changed one Sunday morning. Very unusually for me, I tuned into the local radio station, BRMB, my favourite radio station being radio three as you would expect. As I was reading the paper I heard the DJ say that he was going to interview a member of the Birmingham Gay Switchboard after the next disc. I put down the paper, turned up the volume, and listened. The DJ introduced a man called Joe, who went on to explain the roll of the switchboard and to say anyone was welcome to phone with any problems or questions that they might have. When you consider that today there are a huge range of websites and chat rooms dedicated to gay life, and the various problems that gay men and women still encounter today; none of this existed in the seventies, and the switchboard provided a huge amount of support in what was still a hostile world for homosexuals. These switchboards operated all over the country, the largest being in London, where Joe had done his training. As I listened I could see that this could be the answer to my problem. At the end of the interview, Joe gave the number of the switchboard which I hastily wrote down.

Just outside my flat there was a public telephone and that evening, armed with lots of change, I dialled the number given that morning. The phone was answered by a pleasant sounding young man. I told him who I was and said that I was new to the scene and could he tell me where the best gay bars were to be found in Birmingham. He was very helpful, but the thought came to me that to get to know the scene properly, it would be better to be introduced to it by someone who knew it really well. I asked if would be possible to meet someone, and I suggested Joe. Understandably he was very cautious, after all, I could have been some kind of homophobic head case, who wanted to cause harm to someone involved in the switchboard. I was very reasonable and managed to convince him of my genuineness. He asked me to call back in half-an-hour and he'd see what he could do. When I called him he told me that he'd spoken to Joe and could I go over to an address in Moseley the next afternoon. As I was on my rest days from the bank, I readily agreed while hastily writing down the address. Large numbers of the large, Victorian houses in Moseley had been converted into flats by this time and were inhabited by students studying at Birmingham University. I rang the bell and waited.

The door was answered by a tall, slim, bearded man in his early thirties I guessed. He gave me a warm smile shaking my hand as I introduced myself. I was immediately struck by his warmth and openness, and as I got to know him well over the coming months, I learned that he was a preacher with the 'Metropolitan Community Church'. The MCC was a church with its origins in America, and it gave a welcome to gay men and women who felt excluded from the mainstream churches. And, I'm sad to say, they usually were at that time. When I walked into the flat there was another chap sitting there who Joe introduced as Sam. Younger than Joe, I learned that he was a mature student studying at the university. I later was to learn that Sam was a leading light in the 'Gay Liberation Front' movement, and as you'll guess by the name, Bill, was an extremely left-wing organisation. I spent the next couple of hours talking about myself and the problems that I'd encountered in the army, a subject that they knew absolutely nothing about. They invited me to a night out at a well known Birmingham gay pub called 'The Jester,' a place that quickly became my second home. It was truly wonderful for me to at last be in a place where I could be myself, and it was almost exclusively gay.

That first night in the Jester, Joe and Sam introduced me to a number of young men, most of whom were students, with long flowing locks and many with a far away look in their eyes, no doubt the result of copious amounts of marijuana. I also noticed that many of them were wearing badges saying that they were 'Glad to be Gay', and I remember thinking how incredibly brave they were, giving a two-fingered salute to the world. The gays were at last out of the closet, and God help anyone who tried to shove them back in again. By this time, gay bars and clubs were springing up all over the country, as gay men, no longer criminalised by the state started to flex their muscles. I did admire them, but many of them looked at me with a certain amount of suspicion. I think that they saw me as being too 'establishment' for their taste, especially when they learned that I worked for that pillar of the capitalist world, 'The Bank of England'. I was later to learn all about this left-wing group the 'Gay Liberation Front', the name should give you a clue, over the coming months and while I couldn't help but admire their determination, I sensed their contempt for anyone who didn't share their extreme and often violent methods. Some months later, after I'd met Martin, we invited a group from 'Friend' which included some of these young, GLF men to a party at our home in Ampton road. Standing over in a corner of the room I noticed a group of them looking around enviously at our possessions, while at the same time swigging large amounts of lager. At the end of the night, while clearing up, we looked in horror at a ruined mahogany table, the once glossy surface now covered in cigarette burns which had been used by them as an ash tray during the course of the party. They obviously saw us as posh 'toffs' and 'respectable homosexuals', the 'Uncle Toms' of the gay world. Perhaps that's where I get my intense dislike of left-wing politics from? Not that I cared that night in the the Jester as all of this was to come some time in the future. I was just delighted to be surrounded by happy gay men, all bent on having a good time. When you consider that this was only eight years after the partial decriminalisation of homosexuality in Britain, the fall out was huge, and starting to gain momentum and a life of its own.

I did meet a young student called Neil. He was tall, clean shaven and came from Somerset. We embarked on a brief affair but as we had nothing much in common, it wasn't going to go anywhere and quickly fizzled out. I have very fond memories of the Jester which is still going strong today. Whenever I hear the ABBA song, 'Dancing Queen', which was played endlessly, my thoughts go back to the very many happy liberated hours that I spent there. In just about a year, a whole new and exciting world had opened up to me and I was extremely grateful to Joe for introducing me to it. It would have been easy to find out about the various gay aspects of the Birmingham gay scene without Joe's help, but I would have still been alone and isolated by not knowing anyone.

This would be a very good time to get back briefly to a subject mentioned by me much earlier in this letter to you both. The idea of the 'respectable homosexual'. This idea first surfaced as early as the 1920s, when certain academics and members of the medical profession started to question the criminalisation of large numbers of men simply for being 'different'. They argued that as long as a man led a quiet and respectable life, it was no business of the state how they led their private lives behind closed doors. The key to the argument was being, 'respectable' and homosexuals who spent their time consorting with the 'low-lifes' who inhabited disreputable pubs, public toilets, and open spaces for sexual purposes, should be excluded. A number of high profile gay men, including John Gielgud, Lord Montague, and Peter Wildeblood, had been prosecuted for sexual offences and questions started to be asked as to whether these prosecutions were strictly necessary by newspapers such as *The Observer* and *New Statesman*. They demanded a 'reasoned discussion on homosexuality', drawing upon progressive medical and legal opinion. In 1954, a committee was set up by the then Home Secretary, David Maxwell-Fyfe, and headed by John Wolfenden, to look into the whole subject of homosexuality. A number of these 'respectable homosexuals' were interviewed by Wolfenden who often sat down to cosy lunches in London gentlemen's clubs to discuss the matter with them. Wolfenden did not once talk to any gay man who'd fallen foul of the law for cottaging or having sex in public spaces though. And people like Wildeblood were less than candid as to how they first met their partners, many of whom had met them in places that they were now ready to condemn as unsavoury and disreputable. I believe that John Gielgud for example, had been prosecuted for cottaging. I don't intend to go into this whole subject in any great detail here, but in 1957, Wolfenden recommended a partial decriminalisation of homosexual acts between men over twenty-one, and in the privacy of their own homes. And as you know, the law was finally changed to that effect in 1967.

It could be said that without the 'respectable homosexuals' arguments, the change in the law would have taken far longer than the time that it did. It's certainly true to say that the majority of gay men avoided the less savoury aspects of gay life, not for any moral reasons but simply because it was to dangerous to do so. You could say that Martin and I came under the category of the 'respectable homosexual', but only in the sense that we had no interest in either cottaging, or having sex with strangers in public spaces. For the rest, we embraced the whole of the gay scene with open arms and had a whale of a time during our early years together, but more of that later. It's now only in old age that we no longer go to any gay venues, preferring to leave it to the young who have the stamina for it. I can give you an example of the changes in the law in 1967 and the age of consent being fixed at twenty-one. We had a friend called David who owned two stationary shops in the Birmingham area. He fell in love with and started an affair with a young man called Stephen, who was at that time twenty years old. They were deeply in love and Stephen begged David to let him move in with him. David refused, saying that on Stephen's twenty-first birthday they could start living openly together but not before, which is what they did. David was of course right, as he risked prosecution for having under-age sex. This seems absurd to us today given that Stephen was twenty years old and could hardly be described as a minor, but to David it was a very real threat which he had to take seriously.

As I've said to you both all along, for me the most important thing was the decriminalisation that the change in 1967 bought, and that further changes would automatically come over the passage of time. Which is exactly what happened. Once the genie had been let out of the bottle ever more changes would be demanded, until homosexuals were given the same rights as everyone else in British society. I for one have never demanded 'special treatment', but I do want to be treated as an equal in the sight of the law. If anyone back in 1975 had said that gay men would eventually have the right of civil partnership for example, I would have laughed at them and said 'never in my lifetime'. I'm glad to say that I've been proved wrong on all counts.

Just before Christmas in 1976, the tenth of December to be precise, I was sitting in the Jester early one evening and met the young man who was to change my life for ever. A short time after I'd settled in Birmingham and after I'd met Joe, I started to work on Gay Switchboard after some training from Joe. After their kindness towards me and with a feeling of 'giving something back', I decided to volunteer, and given my past experiences, I felt that I had a lot to offer. Joe agreed, and I was welcomed with open arms. The reason that I mention this now is that a chap called Stephen, who was the treasurer of the newly opened gay centre, which was home to gay switchboard, was with the handsome young man, and a chap called John, Stephen's partner, who came into the pub that night. They sat down together on the far side of the room and as I sipped my pint, I tried to pluck up the courage to join them. Martin was tall and slim with brown, wavy hair and to me, was incredibly handsome. At that moment I fell deeply in love with him and was determined that before the night was out, I was going to get to know him better, although I doubted that he'd take much notice of me. I strolled across towards them and noticed that Martin watched my progress across the room with interest. I smiled at Stephen and John, said hello, and asked if I could join them. I quickly introduced myself to Martin and the four of us fell into conversation. I learned that Martin was an English teacher at comprehensive school, and that he'd been a pupil there when it was still a grammar school. We quickly discovered a mutual love of music and art, and I was impressed at his knowledge of English religious choral music, which was far better than mine. I should explain that Martin and Stephen had been at school together and had been good friends. One evening Stephen had told Martin that he was gay, and Martin had admitted that he was too. Both of them shared a bond. Stephen and John lived in a large, Victorian house in the then highly desirable district of Edgbaston, and that Martin was their next door neighbour. John was a very nice guy and was much less serious than Stephen, who came across as being rather pedantic and who took himself very seriously indeed. As the night progressed and I relaxed a little we became more animated, and talked about all kinds of subjects. I couldn't keep my eyes off Martin and was encouraged when I felt his eyes on me when he thought that I wasn't looking. As the bell rang for last orders, I realized that if I didn't make a move soon, then he'd be gone and the moment would be lost. As we all stood to leave, I turned to Martin and hesitatingly asked if he would like to join me for dinner one night. To my great relief and joy, he said that he'd love to and when and where could we meet. As John looked on beaming, and while Stephen regarded me with something like suspicion, we agreed to meet at a restaurant just around the corner from the Jester called Cassidy's, a gay owned and friendly place, on the coming Friday. With my heart singing with joy, I took the bus home to my studio in Erdington.

I'll never forget waiting outside the restaurant that night. I kept nervously glancing at my watch wondering if Martin would turn up or if he'd changed his mind. I felt full of self-doubt asking myself would a well educated young man have any interest me. I needn't have worried. I quickly sensed as we sat down together that he was genuinely interested in me, and my previous life and problems with the army. Martin and I came from remarkably similar backgrounds, both coming from working-class families, our mothers even been born within two streets of each other in back-to-backs in Ladywood.

We talked for hours over dinner and he confided that the only reason he'd gone to the Jester was because Stephen had been badgering him to do so for months, so he finally gave in. Personally I thank God that he did. After we'd finished and paid the bill, he turned to me and asked if I'd like to go back to his flat, and of course I immediately accepted. That night, Martin and I fell deeply in love, a love that's endured for almost forty years now. In the early days I admit that I wasn't the easiest person to live with, being unused to giving and receiving such deep affection. I think that It's testament to the deep love that we have for each other, that we were able to overcome our problems and move forward together. To my mind, one of the saddest aspects of gay life is the transience of many gay relationships, which seem to last a short period before one or the other of the couple moves on to yet another transient relationship. Martin and I are certainly a minority within a minority. Within days, we started to seriously talk about living together. I don't remember now who first bought up the subject but both agreed that it was what we wanted, and after Martin had OK'd it with the estate manager, I started to pack my few belongings. Stephen of course was horrified, telling Martin in no uncertain terms that he thought that he was mad and that he knew nothing about me. And while that was true, we were both confident enough to make it work. And so, just before Christmas 1976, I moved in. I still marvel that I'd only been out of the army for eighteen months by this time and already my life had changed beyond all recognition.

The Christmas that followed was the happiest of my adult life. It seems to have stretched out endlessly and it was at this time that we both met our respective parents. The first to arrive was Martin's mother and father, who were due to go off to St Anne's-on-Sea for their Christmas holiday. I made sure that I was smartly dressed, even wearing my regimental blazer after been told by Martin that his dad was an old soldier and active in the RBL. It proved to be a good move on my part. Stephen and Beatty Jackson duly turned up in time for a cup of tea, and I set about trying to be as charming as I knew how. Stephen was a stiff-backed man, and very much the old soldier being a veteran of the war. He was a very serious kind of chap and very old- fashioned, who disliked drinking and bad language. In fact he was very much like my own dad in that respect as they were both of the same generation and similar backgrounds. Steve and I hit off immediately and we always had a good relationship over the coming years. Martin's mother, known as Beatty, was more cautious. Martin was after all her youngest son and clearly her favourite, and it was to take her much longer to get used to my appearance in Martin's life. Although it was never discussed, they both must have guessed the truth about us both. Something that for people of their generation was still very hard to accept. Martin was also four years younger than I was being only twenty-four at the time, which must have seemed a big gap to them. But there were never any recriminations and as they realised that Martin was genuinely happy, they seemed to accept the situation. After they left, we headed out to buy a Christmas tree which we took great delight in decorating. I remember the feeling of utter contentment as we sat together that evening listening to Vaughan Williams' 'The Lark Ascending', a piece that was new to me.

We enjoyed a Christmas lunch together and started to think about the Spencer clan's visit on Boxing day. My mother, being a bit of a snob, I knew would be very impressed with our home. It was a large, Victorian house on the Calthorpe Estate. The Calthorpe's, a hugely wealthy family owned large swathes of Edgbaston, and rented their properties out at very reasonable rates. We had a large living room with high a ceiling and impressive original, marble fire place, and Martin, who was extremely artistic, had furnished the room with exquisite taste. We had a kitchen, which had originally been the master's dressing-room, and a large bedroom. We'd had a large double bed delivered just before Christmas as sleeping in Martin's old single had been a bit uncomfortable. The only slight drawback was that the bathroom was just down the corridor, not that that bothered us very much. Living next door, was a delightful, cherubic old lady called Katy Kettle, who had an enormous old tabby cat who was so fat that it could barely walk. On the ground floor lived Jock and Nella. Nella was a blue-rinsed lady and very proper, while old Jock had been a prisoner of the Germans during the great war, and liked to show off his scar, the result of a German bayonet. Up above, in what used to be the servants' bedrooms, lived a delightful young couple called Karen and Ashley, and Martin and I had trouble keeping our lustful eyes off him. Not that he seemed to mind, as on one occasion, after being called to the telephone by Martin, he arrived dripping wet and with a towel wrapped around his waist. He'd been under the shower when Martin had called him down. This delightfully laid-back attitude gives a good insight into the way that people's views were beginning to change, most especially young people. I can give you many examples of this from those days. If you remember I mentioned the young man from the Prudential, and there were a number of occasions, when, without in any way hiding my sexuality, was openly admiring of attractive young men who I happened to meet. They almost always smiled, knowing full well that I fancied them while going on to mention their current girlfriend.

Anyway, back to Christmas. My mother and father, younger sister and boyfriend, now her husband, my elder brother and his wife, all arrived on Boxing day evening. My mother instantly going into raptures about the place, while my dad looked at me with a look of approval on his face, no doubt his mind dwelling on the events of only a few months previously. I can safely say that the whole family fell instantly in love with Martin. Mom gave him a hug, and said,

'Welcome to the family, Martin, It's like discovering another son'. It was a wonderful night and everyone embraced Martin and continue to love him to this day.

As we went into 1977 I started to have a niggle that would not go away no matter how much I tried to force it into the back of my mind. I still hadn't come out as gay at the bank. I anguished over it constantly. The bank represented the 'Establishment' and could I trust them to give me a fair deal, or would they do all in their power to some how force me out. After my encounter with the army, I distrusted any kind of official establishment and viewed them all with suspicion. Don't forget it had only been ten years since the change in the law, and the world could still be a very hostile place for gay men back then. I talked it over endlessly with Martin and finally made my decision one Sunday evening. Walking into the bank the next day I was consumed with fear and almost changed my mind. The security staff had their own room and we'd congregate there for coffee before starting work. With my heart beating like a trip hammer I said that there was something that I'd like to tell them. They fell silent, all looking towards me expectantly. Of course I can't now remember my exact words but I quietly said something along the lines of, that I was gay and that I was living with a young man called Martin. I continued by saying that I hoped that this news wouldn't make any difference to them and that we could continue to work together. I fell silent and looked around at their stunned expressions. It seemed like an age before someone actually said something. The silence was finally broken by a chap called Mike. Mike and I had become good pals and would usually go and have a pint together during the lunch break. In fact most of us security men spent an hour together in the pub at lunch time and we all got along well. I hoped that that wasn't about to change. Mike looked at me, shrugged and said, 'So what, your private life is your own affair, Dave, and has nothing to do with the rest of us.' He paused for a second and continued, 'But thanks for telling us, it was a brave thing to do'. One of the old naval men tried to lighten the situation by saying with a grin, 'Just as long as you don't pinch me bum when we're on nights'. Everyone laughed and with a huge rush of relief I left the table and prepared for work.

So far, so good, I thought to myself, but what about the official reaction. My immediate boss was a man called Brian. Brian had done his national service in the Grenadier Guards, and we got along well. He could always be found in the pub at lunch times and would always buy the lads a drink. When I came back for coffee break that morning, Brian was waiting for me and immediately launched into a tirade against the 'poofs and queers' etc. He was very angry, and I thought just a bit *too* angry. My fists clenched and I was more than ready to defend myself if the need arose. Mike, who, was a great pal of Brian's, shoved Brian out of the room and into his office and things quietened down. Another chap, an Irish Catholic called Kevin, came over to me that day and said quietly, 'Dave, I can never agree with your way of life, but that doesn't mean that I can't work with you.' He continued by saying, 'What you did this morning took a lot of courage and I admire you for that'. I thanked him and we shook hands. But what of Brian, ah, Brian. I've long had my own theory as to why Brian reacted in the way that he did that morning. I've often wondered if Brian was one of those young guardsmen who had the occasional fling with a 'special gentleman friend' while stationed in London in the '50s, and to be honest, it wouldn't surprise me if he had in the least. Brian's storm very quickly passed and we were soon back on speaking terms, almost as if nothing had ever happened.

And the official reaction wasn't long in coming either. I think it was the next day when Brian came in while we were having coffee, and announced that we were to have an important visitor the next day. Back then, the bank always employed a very senior ex-police officer as their head of security. Brian told us that this man was to visit the security staff the next day and I knew why. By this time I was quite laid-back about the whole thing as I reasoned that the worse part was already over. The big boss arrived the next morning and straight away took over Brian's office. I can't remember his name now, but do have a recollection that he'd been the man who led the Cannock Chase' murder investigation. We all sat around waiting to be called in and before long it was my turn. This, of course, was a charade. The only reason that this man came up from London was to see me and none other. I knocked the door and walked in to be faced by a well dressed, middle-aged man. He invited me to sit down and without wasting any time mentioned the previous days events, when I'd come out as gay. I said that yes, that was correct. I think that he asked why I'd come out, and I replied that I was no longer prepared to live a lie, especially now that I was in a serious relationship. And I politely pointed out that homosexuality was no longer a crime in Britain. Our conversation was both friendly and polite. After I 'd finished speaking, he carried on by saying, 'Well, now that you've come out, you can't be regarded as a security risk'. At that moment I saw red, rarely having felt so angry before or since. I tensed my body, and looking him straight in the eye, I said, through gritted teeth, 'I have never, ever been a security risk.' Giving me a broad smile and nodding his head, he sat back in his chair and quietly thanked me. He seemed completely satisfied and from then on the matter was dropped. I'd won a small victory. And you can't believe how important that victory was to me.

In the days and weeks that followed I became something of a hero, especially with the young, female staff. God only knows why, but everyone went out of their way to show their support. I was rather put out, though, when one morning, one of our cleaning ladies, an elderly, working-class Brummie, asked me who took the dominant role in the bedroom. I was speechless but did see the funny side of it. However, I can't for the life of me remember how I answered the question. For the second time in less than two years, I felt as if a huge weight had been lifted off my shoulders. No more lies, no more pretence. It became perfectly normal from then on to talk of my life in the same way that my straight colleagues talked about their own. I was often asked how Martin was and what we'd done together over the weekend, just normal everyday stuff. When I look back now, I think that I was brave to do what I did that day, and although attitudes were slowly beginning to change in Britain it was still early days, and there could have been an unfavourable reaction, especially from the other men. I think that I was a bit ahead of my time, but don't regret my decision for a minute.

10

Gay Hotels, Bars and Clubs, and How We Enjoyed Ourselves Rather Like Kids in a Sweetshop

Saturday night was the highlight of our week. After watching the latest episode of 'Dallas', a hugely popular American soap, Martin and I put on our glad-rags and headed out to the then most popular gay venue in Birmingham, 'The Grosvenor'. When you consider that it had barely been ten years since partial decriminalisation, the explosion of gay clubs, bars, and hotels was remarkable. There was a very good magazine then in print called 'Gay Times'. It was a serious magazine which covered all aspects of gay life and the many issues that were of interest or concern to gay men at that time. If you turned to the back, there were pages of adverts for gay hotels and bars, which were dotted all over the country. The competition between these various businesses was fierce and the standards were high.

Martin and I, who were both very unworldly when it came to many aspects of gay life, embraced it all and went on a voyage of discovery. The Grosvenor was situated along the Hagley Road in Edgbaston, and was set back off the road. A large Victorian pile, it had hotel accommodation, an outdoor pool and restaurant, three bars, and a quiet room with a large, grand piano. On a typical Saturday night, it was often standing room only, with a mixture of age groups, from the old 'queens' of the forties generation, to the modern young gay, who gave a finger to a still largely hostile society. Late on a Saturday night, you could often find the older clientèle standing around the piano singing songs from the musicals, while the younger ones gyrated to the loud disco music in the other room. Everyone got on well together, and the reason that these places thrived at this time was simply because people could be themselves, without continually having to look over their shoulders. The place was so popular that getting a taxi home in the early hours of a Saturday morning was a nightmare, usually involving a long wait.

Martin and I spent many happy hours there over the following years and we even took my younger sister, and her then new husband, with us on one occasion. One Saturday night, we were both sitting in the bar having a drink when I noticed a look of surprise and alarm cross Martin's features. Following his gaze I looked over towards the bar and noticed two very young and attractive boys walking in. I say boys as they couldn't have been more than sixteen, and I wondered how they'd managed to slip in past the doormen. In fact they were fifteen, in the sixth form at his school and Martin taught them English. I could see that he was concerned about this. Like many gay men who had responsibility for the young in those days, it was not a good idea to advertise the fact that you were gay, yes, the world was changing, but not by that much. Still, to many people, homosexual equalled paedophile, and they were horrified at the thought that their children would become corrupted, or victims of abuse from those who were responsible for them. As is now coming to light, the sexual abuse of children seems to have been widespread back in the 1970s and 1980s in many institutions, and although Martin would no more think of abusing a boy than most other gay men, he was sensible enough to know that he was vulnerable to an accusation of that kind had his sexuality come to light. Sadly, there were many decent men in his position at that time, but all tarred with the same brush in the eyes of many. And as far as sexual abuse goes back then, I think that there's a ticking bomb just waiting to go off, and when it does, the fallout will be horrendous. I believe that there are many men in very high places, walking around today who are living in fear that their crimes are about to be exposed.

The two lads, both looking very sheepish, sat at a table as far away as possible from us. We both ignored them, and after a short while, they both left. I could tell that Martin was worried about this, and my telling him that he wasn't doing anything illegal didn't help matters, as if that made any difference. As it happens he needn't have worried. I'm sure that the two boys concerned were terrified that if they were found out as having been in such a place, they would have found themselves in a great deal of trouble. So they kept their mouths firmly shut, hoping that Martin would do exactly the same, which of course he did. The Jester also remained a firm favourite and we often went there during the week for a few beers.

Gay hotels were another interesting phenomenon. They blossomed during the 1970s, 1980s, and 1990s, but have now just about vanished. As I'm sure you're aware, no hotel today could advertise itself as being exclusively gay, as that would be discriminatory, and therefore illegal. The recent case of the two 'Christian' hotel owners highlights this point. They refused a gay couple a double room because they were homosexual and unmarried, and as a result, the gay men took them to court on the grounds of discrimination and won their case. This would be an identical situation if a gay hotel refused a room to a heterosexual couple. This was not the case back then.

The reason that gay hotels flourished was simple. Homosexuals were unwelcome in main stream hotels and once it was realised that they were gay they came in for a great deal of hostility from the other hotel guests. I've lost count of the number of times that Martin and I experienced this kind of homophobic behaviour, and it's a miracle to me that I was able to keep my temper in check and didn't physically assault someone. No one ever actually said anything, but their dislike was clearly etched over their faces mean, vindictive faces. So what did we do? Like countless thousands of others, we voted with our feet, arguing why should we give large amounts of money to people who despised us. The gay hotel flourished in those years, not only in the UK but worldwide. There was a popular guide published in Germany called 'The Spartacus Gay Guide,' and it was a must for the gay traveller. Martin and I always had an up to date copy and never went anywhere without it. It was a thick publication as you can imagine, and listed country by country and city by city the many hotels, bars and clubs, all being given a star rating rather like an AA guide. In the USA they published their own version.

In Britain, the seaside hotels were particularly popular, but more tranquil locations in the Lake district and such places could be found. As I said earlier, these hotels and guest houses were of a very high standard. And the gay holiday-maker was more than happy to pay a good price to stay at such places, where they knew that they were welcome. The 'pink pound' as it came to be known carried a lot of weight. The 'normal' tourist trade must have lost a fortune over the years, something that I'm very glad about. There was a hotel in Torquay called 'Cliff House' that was very popular and Martin and I stayed there on very many occasions over twenty years. Set in its own grounds, with outdoor swimming pool and sauna, the hotel was known worldwide and was usually fully booked during the summer months. The atmosphere was relaxed and friendly, and the hotel bar was the place that everyone congregated in the evenings. The sauna was always busy and widely used by guests and people coming in from the outside. We spent many happy holidays their over the years.

London had a very large number of hotels and guest houses used by tourists and English gays alike, and these were always within easy walking distance to the various bars and clubs that were dotted all over the capital at the time. It's unfortunate that a gay hotel called the 'Elm Guest House' has come to public attention just recently. This place appears to have been used by a group of paedophiles to sexually abuse young boys, many of whom were in care. All of the abusers seem to have been high profile men, and it's almost certain that there's been a wide spread cover up to protect them. Again, I believe that this is another bomb quietly ticking away which is about to explode. I can only speak though from my own personal experience. In all of the years that we used gay hotels in the UK, I never witnessed anything that could be termed as inappropriate in any of the places that we stayed in. I believe that the vast majority of these hotels were well run, and that no responsible owner would allow their premises to be used for illegal activity. After all, they were in business and had a lot to lose had they come under investigation by the police. By the mid-1990s and going into middle-age, Martin and I stopped using gay hotels; we had no need to and by that time the atmosphere had changed in the hotel world and discrimination had largely disappeared. Also, we were financially more able to afford the services of the high end hotel market. Some time ago we met two very old friends of ours who'd stayed at Cliff House countless times over more than thirty years. They sadly announced that their previous visit to the hotel was to be their last. They described the place as being run down, dirty, and seedy, a shadow of its former self. These two, now very elderly men, who knew well the discrimination of the forties and fifties, seemed lost and sad as they remembered the happy times that they'd spent there, knowing in their hearts that era of the gay hotel time has now gone forever.

The history of the gay hotel is a relatively short one, but they were places where gay men could relax and be their real selves in what was still a still largely hostile world. We recently spoke to two gay owners of a beautiful country house near to Bath. It used to be exclusively gay, but now welcomes a mixture of guests both gay and straight and no matter what their sexual orientation, everyone seems to get along together well.

11

Amsterdam:
Where the Sweetshop Was Always Open

On most Friday afternoons in the late 1970s, if you boarded the early afternoon flight to Amsterdam from Birmingham, you couldn't help but notice that the vast majority of the passengers were young men. Amsterdam back then was the Mecca of gay freedoms still unknown in Britain, and this was where gay men young, and not so young, headed for a weekend of pleasure. The prophets of the old testament would have had a field day condemning this modern day 'Sodom'. Lively and vibrant, just about everything that a gay man could possibly want was available twenty-four hours a day. Countless gay hotels provided accommodation in the heart of the gay quarter. All that you needed to do was walk out of your hotel, and within a few paces you could walk into one of the many gay bars on either side of the street These bars catered to all tastes, whether it be, leather and S&M, usually frequented by muscular, butch types with shaven heads, bushy moustaches and tattoos, to transvestite bars, no need to describe the favourite mode of dress there, to the bars frequented by the young, pretty, fey types. Had Oscar Wilde and 'Bosie' lived to see it, they would have thought that they'd died and gone to paradise. Martin and I were frequent visitors to the city and almost always stayed in a gay hotel called 'The Unique', although we did stay in others including 'The Queens Head' and 'The New York'. Our first visit was in 1978 and we went there regularly well into the 1980s. I can't adequately describe to you, John and Bill, how Martin and I were totally amazed and blown away by the place on our first visit.

Nothing like it existed in Britain at that time, not at all surprising when you consider that only ten years previously, homosexuality had still been illegal in our 'enlightened democracy'. And yet barely an hours flight from the UK, was this wonderfully vibrant city where the attitude was 'live and let live'. We could hardly credit that we inhabited the same planet.

Just up the street from our hotel was another hotel called 'The Orfeo', and within the hotel complex was a gay sex shop and cinema. The manager of the sex shop was a plump, jolly Amsterdamer called Fred. We became great friends with Fred over the next twenty years, and we often went for a meal or drink together. The shop sold all kinds of things that are better not described here, but the shelves were groaning with gay pornographic magazines and videos. If you joined the video club, you could rent the latest porn, usually from America, and return it the next day. The videos were also for sale of course, but were not cheap, costing on average about £100 pounds in 1980. That must be at least £300 at today's prices. Incidentally, I think that a porn DVD now costs about £25, a huge reduction. It's not surprising when you consider the vast number of studios producing this stuff, and the competition is fierce thus keeping down the cost. You may well ask how I know all of this. As just about everything today, all that you need to do is take a look on the internet.

The Orfeo cinema was always full, with a selection of films continually showing on a loop. The programme was changed every twenty-four hours. Amsterdam was full of such places catering for both gay and straight clientèle, but Amsterdam was not exclusive in its huge sex industry. Anyone who served with BAOR for example, knew of sex shops selling much of the same type of stuff in the large cities of Germany. It's only in Britain where such shops were outlawed, and the few that existed were constantly being raided by the police and closed down, only to reopen a few days later, once again fully stocked. You can of course take a moral view on the subject, which is something that I'm trying to avoid, but these sex shops in the many European Cities, were operating quite legally and their products were not illegal. I can tell you that even little Catholic Luxembourg City had at least three sex shops and maybe more.

Fred often told us of the many gay English customers who bought a video or two and asked Fred to get rid of the boxes from them, which he was happy to do. They would then go and buy a Walt Disney video of Snow White, or something like that, then insert the porn into the Disney box in the hope of fooling HM Customs & Excise on their return to the UK. This was risky, as the customs men weren't stupid and knew all of the tricks, and if caught, you could at best expect to have the offending item confiscated, but at worst be prosecuted for importing pornography into the UK. As we all know, the pendulum has now swung the other way, and pornography is now widely available for sale on the internet. I'm talking about the 'legal' porn, that is where the people taking part are eighteen or over, and the various studios all mark their products, 'proof on file'.

Martin and I also once paid a visit to a well known, Amsterdam gay brothel, but not as clients I hasten to add. We stood at the busy bar one evening having a drink and looking around at, it has to be said, the extremely attractive and scantily clad young men who were readily available, for the right price of course. One of these young men approached us and started chatting. He was about twenty, with blond, wavy hair, and was of Dutch nationality. He was obviously hoping that we'd buy him a drink or more, but when he realised that we were simply there out of curiosity he quickly left, looking for more promising clients. I do know that live sex shows were also a regular feature of the place provided that there were enough people there that night who were prepared to pay the hefty entrance fee. I'm not setting out to shock or outrage you in reporting this but am simply giving you a true picture of Amsterdam gay life as it was in the late 1970s. It's no doubt still the same today. Any moral judgements I leave up to yourselves. After leaving England in 1980, Martin and I used to visit Amsterdam often and spent some happy times there. However, in later years and as we started to get older, we always stayed at a five star central hotel called' 'The Ambassade', which cost a fortune but was more suited to our needs. We often liked to get away from Luxembourg between Christmas and the new year, and we'd usually head to Amsterdam, a relatively simple rail journey.

There is an amusing story to tell about a stay in the hotel 'New York', another well known Amsterdam gay hotel. The large breakfast room was in the reception area. One morning we were sitting having breakfast, when three young, and typical English football fans sauntered in wearing their 'bovver' boots, shaven heads, tight jeans, and team scarves. All heads turned towards them as they approached reception, totally oblivious to their surroundings. There was an England versus Holland match on that night and I imagine that hotel space was at a premium in the city. The owner of the hotel who was on reception, smiled and raised his head as one asked if he had a room for that night. He said, yes, certainly, before continuing, 'You do realise, don't you, that this hotel is exclusively gay, but you're certainly welcome to stay if you want'. All heads were raised as we waited to hear what they would say. There was a pause as they looked at each other, all starting to go slightly red in the face, until one of them said, 'F*** that!' They abruptly turned and headed for the entrance far quicker than when they'd first entered, muttering darkly about f****** queers, closely followed by the chuckles and, it has to be said, admiring glances of the assembled breakfast-goers.

We also travelled to various European cities armed with our Spartacus Guide, which came in useful in searching out the local gay scene. Of course, as we got older and entered middle-age, the attractions that we found so exiting in our youth became far less interesting and the thought of being in some gay bar in the early hours of the morning quickly paled. But, being English, Amsterdam was a place that was so relaxed about sex and sexuality, it's no great surprise that so many gay men of our generation found the place so liberating.

Today, no gay person needs to get on a flight out of the country to find the attractions that were only available in Amsterdam in the 1980s, as they are here right on the doorstep. London, and Manchester offer everything that I've described above. I believe that the 'in place' for the weekender now is Prague, where the gay scene is as vibrant as it ever was in our younger days in the Dutch city. Just out of interest I looked on google recently, and I could only find three Amsterdam hotels that advertised themselves as being exclusively gay.

There is one very important thing that I haven't yet mentioned in this letter to you both, and that is the AIDS epidemic that swept the world in the early eighties. I'm ashamed to say that as I was never remotely affected by AIDS I tend to ignore it and the devastating effect it had on homosexuals. Conspiracy theories abound as to just how the virus first appeared and where it came from, one favourite being that it had been manufactured in some laboratory somewhere by the CIA, but no one seems to know for sure. Many so called 'Christians' rubbed their hands with glee and declared it to be God's judgement on the world's 'sodomites'. But what of the reaction of the British government of the day? That can be summed up in one word: 'shameful'. The Conservative government, led by Margaret Thatcher did nothing. Music to your ears, eh, Bill? I had the distinct impression at the time that their attitude was 'so what? It's only killing queers'. That piece of toilet paper, *The Sun* had a field day with bold headlines using the words 'poof and queers' on a regular basis, and they weren't alone. I remember reading a book by the gay rights campaigner Peter Tatchel written in the early eighties. Peter Tatchel is man for whom I have a huge amount of respect. For most of his life he's fought tooth and nail for gay rights often putting his life in danger. He's never once backed down, and has had to turn his house into a fortress to protect himself from his numerous enemies. Campaigning around the world for gay rights, he's been badly beaten up so many times that he's lost count, Russia being just one of these many countries. To me, he's a man of immense courage, but will never be given the recognition that he deserves.

In the book that he wrote, Tatchel told the story of a well known gay club in London. Seeing that nothing was being done to alert homosexuals to the grave dangers that they faced from the AIDS virus by the authorities, the clubs committee decided to do something to educate their gay members. They had a large number of pamphlets produced at their own expense, these were, I believe, also widely distributed around other gay venues in the city. The pamphlets were extremely explicit. The group argued that given the nature of the epidemic, it was essential that the material was as hard- hitting as possible, and so were designed to shock. So what happened? One night the club was raided by the police, along with others, and all of the pamphlets were confiscated and destroyed. I think that the reason given at the time is that were obscene, or some such official excuse. Instead of welcoming this self-help campaign, the government of the day did everything in their power to suppress it. It was only when AIDS started to appear in the wider community, usually through infected blood products, that the government was forced to get off their a**** and do something positive. It was at this time that the very hard-hitting adverts started to appear on national television using the slogan: 'Don't die of ignorance'. Something that the gay club had been trying to do many months before. This is yet another incident, one of so many, that Britain has nothing to be proud of.

12

1979, and Itchy Feet

Life for us continued as normal during the late seventies. I was fully accepted at the bank and no one ever mentioned my coming out episode of a few months previously. In fact Martin and I hosted a number of evenings at Ampton road for my bank colleagues and their wives. I continued working on gay switchboard a couple of evenings a week and also trained as a 'Friend' councillor, a nationwide gay help group. The gay centre was within easy walking distance of Birmingham city centre, in a run down industrial part of the city. There was a working-man's pub just nearby, and I'd often pop in there in the early evening for a drink before starting at the centre. The licensee's son, a very attractive lad of about nineteen, was usually serving behind the bar and I got to know him. After a while he asked where I was going at that time of night in that area. I answered him honestly and said that I was working on gay switchboard. 'Oh, at that gay place around the corner, you mean?' he asked. I told him yes and what I did there. He was genuinely curious and interested, even asking if I was that way inclined myself, to which I of course answered in the affirmative. After that we had a number of chats about homosexuality, and I was struck by how genuinely interested he was on the whole subject. He was in no way hostile and never sneered at gays or our way of life. He seemed to be glad to be better informed on a subject that he knew little about. This made me hopeful for the future.

One evening I was on duty in the telephone room. It was quiet that night and I sat reading a magazine waiting for the phone to ring, when

I heard footsteps coming down the corridor outside. It sounded like someone wearing a pair of high heels. There was a gentle knock on the door and I shouted, 'Come in'. The door opened and a man, he was obviously a man, wearing a long, blond wig, thickly made up face, and tight clinging dress walked in. Hiding my surprise as best as I could, I smiled and said hello. He rather tentatively returned my smile and asked if he could join me , to which I readily agreed. This transvestite told me that his name was John and that he was happily married with two grown up children. A very nice man, he told me that his wife knew all about his cross dressing and was OK with it but insisted that he didn't dress in that way at home. John told me that there were a number of transvestites who spent the odd weekend at a friendly gay hotel, where they were allowed to dress just as they pleased. He told me that he, and none of his friends were homosexual, but were always given a friendly reception in gay places and that's why he was in the centre that night. Was this a case of 'outsiders' looking out for each other? I would like to have talked for longer, but the phone rang and I had to ask him to leave. I never saw him again but have often wondered what happened to him.

On another occasion the phone went one night and I started to talk to a young lad who was in his very early twenties. He told me that he was gay, but had been married since he was eighteen, and had two small children. He told me that he had a job in sales and so travelled around the Midlands by car. Being more or less his own boss, he told me that he'd started 'cottaging', stopping off at different public toilets during the course of the day. This set alarm bells ringing in my head and I warned of the consequences for him should he be picked up by the police, which I thought almost certain sooner or later. I warned him that if caught and prosecuted, the police would make sure that the local press would be tipped off resulting in him been 'outed ' to his local community with the subsequent loss of his job, and almost certainly his marriage. I told him that he needed to be very careful indeed. Being a Friend councillor, I suggested that we meet for a chat. He readily agreed but insisted that our meeting place had no gay connections. This puzzled me as here he was frequenting known gay cottaging places where the chance of exposure was great, but wouldn't allow himself to be seen in a gay bar. We agreed to meet in a local city centre pub which we did the next night. He was a lovely boy, and we chatted for a couple of hours. I told him that the gay club and pub scene was brilliant and far safer than going cottaging, and if he were to see someone that he knew in a gay bar, then it was likely that they would be gay too. I pointed out that the risks he was taking could well end with him having a criminal record, and what of his wife and children, they'd be utterly betrayed. I kept the thought to myself that this is what he was already doing by living a lie, and that his young wife could well be destroyed by the fallout if he were to be discovered. Fortunately, we had a married bisexual councillor who had a young daughter who he often brought to the gay centre with him. As I felt a bit out of my depth with this young man, having never been married, I suggested that he meet the married councillor, to which he readily agreed. As we left the pub that night, I turned and asked him why, knowing that he was gay, had he got married in the first place. Looking me straight in the eye, he said, 'Because that is what was expected of me'. It seems that the fear of being exposed as 'queer', was still as powerful then as it had ever been.

And then there was the time that I confronted the army. One Sunday evening Martin and I were watching the television when the phone rang. Thinking that it was the bank, I got up and answered it, but was surprised to hear the voice of my boss from Friend at the other end. He told me that a young soldier had phoned switchboard that night asking for help. As I was the only one who had any experience with the armed forces would I be prepared to talk to him. Intrigued, I said of course and what did he have in mind. The boy was on leave he said and could he come and see me the next morning. Luckily, I was on my bank rest days and immediately agreed. We arranged that he should take a taxi over to the flat and we could have a long, uninterrupted talk. The lad who arrived the next day was of medium height, and what I would call a typical squaddie, just the same as countless others that had served in any infantry regiment. He was extremely polite and friendly and very thankful that I'd agreed to see him. I sat him down, made some coffee and after both lighting cigarettes, he started to tell me all about himself. He was eighteen he explained and had enlisted, just like me, as a boy entrant aged sixteen. I could have been looking at myself just a few years previously, as he went on to explain how he'd realised that he had deep homosexual feelings since he was about seventeen. Apparently, he'd been going to gay bars whenever he had the chance but had never tried it on with anyone in the army. I interrupted him at this point and said, 'So, no one in the army knows that you're gay'. He confirmed that that was the case, by saying that he wouldn't have dared come out as his mates in his platoon would have made his life a misery. He'd also been terrified that the army would find out about him. I was glad of that as at least the SIB weren't in the picture, not at the moment, that is. He said that he'd been carrying the burden around with him for months and that he'd now met another young, gay man, and that they were deeply in love and wanted to live together. To make matters worse, his father had found out about him somehow and promptly thrown him out of the house telling him never to go back. Firstly, I had to clarify in my own mind that the kid was telling the truth and that this wasn't some kind of a ploy to get out of the army. I was instantly ashamed at the thought, as looking at him, I could tell that he was genuine, extremely distressed and close to tears. Now here was a dilemma. I asked him what exactly he wanted to do. He swallowed hard before saying, 'I have to tell them that I'm queer, Dave', he said, and continued, 'I don't have a choice. I can't go on like this, it's killing me.' My heart went out to him and of course, I perfectly understood his problem. But what to advise?

I thought back to my own difficulties at Bassingbourne and the one person who I turned to for some help. I've never mentioned it before, but the padre at the depot, while certainly not an ally, did give me a sympathetic ear on a number of occasions. To be honest, I was completely in the dark as what best to advise the lad to do as I had no idea what reaction he'd get from the authorities when he came out. Thinking this course was probably the best under the circumstances, that's what I advised him to do. I told him that when he got back to barracks the next day he should go and see the padre. In the meantime, I'd write a letter to him on Friend headed notepaper and explain the situation. At the same time I strongly advised that he should not under any circumstances admit to having any physical sexual relationship whatsoever. I pointed out to him that as a serving member of the armed forces any homosexual activity on his part was a criminal offence, and if he admitted that he'd been sexually active outside of the army it was still illegal. I was worried that if he said that he'd got a boyfriend in 'civvie' street and if the Military Police became involved, he could find himself in trouble. Given my own experiences I think that I was right to advise caution. He was a lovely lad and couldn't thank me enough, and as he left he gave me a huge hug. I just hoped that his faith in me was justified. I knew that he was stationed at the Light Infantry Brigade Depot in Shrewsbury, and I sat down and wrote a letter addressed to the padre. Two days later, I decided to phone the padre and ask if he'd received my letter. I was put straight through, and while the reception wasn't exactly friendly, he did say that he'd got my letter and it had been passed on higher up the chain. I thanked him, wondering just what the outcome would be.

A few weeks later I received a call from my boss at Friend. He was really happy and told me that he'd heard from our young soldier who had told him that he was to be discharged from the army in a few weeks' time. Apparently the lad had been treated well, especially by his Company Sergeant Major, who'd been very sympathetic to his plight. All in all, a good result I think.

On the subject of the army and homosexuality I have an interesting story to tell. Roy Corbishley, one of my oldest army pals and the first to know that I was gay, which he discovered while we were still on boy service, has a son, Christopher. Christopher is gay and one evening in about 2005, his mother, Christine, phoned me. In great excitement she told me that Christopher had a new boyfriend and that he was a sergeant in the Military Police serving with the Special Investigation Branch. I didn't no whether to laugh or cry when I heard that. The armed forces had been dragged kicking and screaming into the twenty-first century, whether they liked it or not.

I wish, John and Bill, that I could say that because of a certain incident, like violent homophobia for instance, Martin and I first seriously thought about leaving the UK, but I can't. It was unrealistic to expect a huge change in society's attitude towards homosexuality, and while change was coming it was slow. We knew about the far more relaxed, live and let live attitudes prevalent in many European countries, and while we were not naïve enough to think that homophobia was non-existent, we felt that perhaps we'd be happier in one of those countries. For my part, it was a dissatisfaction and anger of the many small, but none the less irritating, prejudices that we encountered in everyday life, as described by me earlier and encountered in restaurants and hotels. OK, we could live with it, but why should we? With this in mind, we seriously started to look at what was out there in the wider EEC, as it was then. We contacted a gay group in Brussels and told them what we were looking for, and within a short time we received an invitation to spend a weekend with them. We took the ferry and train one Friday and were warmly welcomed by a small group on our arrival in Brussels. A Belgian couple, one of them the village postmaster, offered us accommodation in their home and we embarked on a very pleasant weekend. They took us to their gay centre that evening and produced a very nice dinner where we got to know the other members of the group. We were immediately struck by how outgoing they were, being completely relaxed and open about their sexuality. After dinner, we all went off for a night on the local gay scene and we certainly didn't encounter any hostility from the general public. As in France, I think that unlike in Britain, both countries had enjoyed far longer periods where homosexuality was in no way illegal. Did you know for instance, that homosexuality in France had been decriminalised in that country in about 1785. That was one hundred years before the Labouchere Amendment of 1885 criminalising homosexual behaviour. Makes you think, doesn't it?

One of the group was the son of a wealthy, and world famous Belgian chocolate maker, and on the Saturday night he took us all to an exclusive Brussels restaurant. Fortunately, he paid the bill. We were waved off from the station on the Sunday morning having enjoyed a truly wonderful weekend, and after having our eyes opened to the possibilities open to us on the continent. We were however, still none the wiser as to just how we could proceed in finding work. That is until fate took a hand.

At work I'd been talking for months about our desire to live abroad and one morning, Jim came in to our rest room and on seeing me told me about an advert that he'd seen in the *Daily Mail*. He told me that the European Court of Justice were looking for two English messengers to work in Luxembourg. My ears went up when he told me that the newspaper was still in the control room. I went straight in there and retrieved it, opening the relevant page with interest. I'll go to my grave believing that Jim and I shared some kind of a link. It was Jim who first pushed me into applying for the job at the bank, and now here he was telling about this job opportunity. If he hadn't have mentioned it I would never have known anything about these two jobs in Luxembourg. Sadly, Jim died of a heart attack in the early 1980s.

In great excitement, I rushed home that evening and showed the paper to Martin who was very interested, much to my relief. We talked at length that evening and both agreed to send off our applications. I did caution Martin though, as I suspected that he was far too highly qualified for a messenger's post. He shrugged his shoulders and said as long as one of us had a job, then what did it matter. This is a good indication of the love that we had for each other, where he was prepared to give everything up to follow me. His chance to find a job within the EU institutions was to come a few years later. There was a snag for me, though. The advert stated that the successful candidate should have a satisfactory knowledge of a second European language. I had none. It was obvious that for such a minor post, you wouldn't be expected to be fluent in another language, but I was sure that they'd expect a certain amount of fluency from any applicant. What I did feel confident about though was my suitability for such a post if only I could overcome the language problem. Being an ex-member of the armed forces with an exemplary military record, plus working for the prestigious Bank of England, I knew that was in with a good chance. I had no intention though of showing them my 'reasons for discharge' page this time. Martin came to my aid as far as the French went. He had an 'O' level in French and often stood in at school to help out the beginners. We embarked on an intensive course in the basics of the language with Martin digging out his exercise books from his own school days.

Although, as we expected, Martin wasn't accepted for the interview, I certainly was, and was asked to report to an office in Kensington Palace Gardens. I was delighted to see that the date was still a few months away as the jury had to be sent over from Luxembourg. This gave me more months to prepare my French. We reckoned that at an interview, and as I wasn't applying for a translator's post, then the questions should be pretty basic and straightforward. We put together a list of questions on, hobbies, food, music, etc. and hoped that this would be enough for me to bluff my way through. Because that's what it was, bluff. Incidentally, on the first day that I walked through the doors of the Court in Luxembourg, I quickly realised that I needed to improve my French, and fast, which of course I did.

In the summer of 1979, we travelled together to London staying the night in a gay hotel in the Cromwell Road, near to the Kensington Palace gardens. Early the next morning, we walked together towards the EC centre and my date with the jury. We stood together for a short while and Martin squeezed my arm, wished me luck, and walked back in the direction of the hotel. I was the first to arrive, and sat nervously outside, waiting. A short time later the door opened and a pleasant middle-aged Englishman put his head around the door and invited me inside. Sitting at the other end of the room behind a table sat two men. The Englishman, Mr Cheshire, introduced me to a Belgian man called Lens, and a German called Burg. Joining the other two, Cheshire sat down and started the proceedings by saying that he too had served in the army for twenty-two years and had finished with the rank of WO1. This helped me relax a bit, and we talked for a short while as the other two looked on. Mr Lens was fluent in English and asked if I thought that I could live happily in a foreign country. Again this question paid off for me as I could say how much I'd enjoyed being in Germany with the army. Up until this point, the German, Manfred Burg, who was later to go on to be a good friend, hadn't said a word. All of a sudden, he asked me a question in French. Urging myself to think and recognising a question about my hobbies I was able to reply reasonably well in that language. I managed quite well until the final question, when I was asked something about the cuisine, which completely flummoxed me. At that point Cheshire stepped in and bought the interview to an end. Manfred and I were to joke about that for years afterwards. Manfred had previously been an officer with the West German border police for many years.

I stood and shook their hands. They then thanked me for attending while Chris Cheshire led me out of the room, telling me that I'd hear from them in due course. I didn't know it at the time of course, but it was at the recommendations of these juries that a candidate's success, or not, was decided. As I strolled back towards the hotel, in my heart, I was absolutely certain that I'd got that job. I don't know why. I walked past a pub and would have loved a large whiskey, but glancing at my watch I realised that it was still only 10 o'clock. When I walked into the hotel, I found the owner vacuuming the reception carpet. He turned it off and asked how I'd got on. With a huge smile on my face, I said to him, 'Martin and I will stay here the night before we leave for Luxembourg'. He smiled and nodded. I was that certain. When I walked into the room Martin looked up in surprise. He'd been writing a postcard and jumped up saying, 'That was quick'. I embraced him and kissed him saying excitedly, 'Martin, I'm sure that I've got it.'

The next few months passed in an absolute agony as I waited for the letter to arrive. However, when the message came it wasn't by letter. I was sitting in the control room at the bank looking at the screens when the phone rang one morning in April of 1980. My pal, Mike, answered it and handed it over to me saying that it was Martin. Now this had never happened before as he'd never phoned me at the bank. Puzzled, I said hello and with great excitement, he told me that he'd just had a telephone call from a Mr Barnet in Luxembourg asking for me, and could I call him back. I wrote down the number and handed the phone back to Mike, saying something like, 'I think that I'm about to be offered a job in Luxembourg'. I phoned Brian in his office and asked if I could make a call to Luxembourg. He said, 'No, why don't you get yourself off and phone with Martin at home'. I gratefully accepted his kind offer and headed home. Martin and I sat together as I dialled the number and was put through to Mr Barnet. He told me that he was from the personnel office at the Court of Justice and that they would like to offer me the job as messenger and was I still interested. Giving Martin a great big smile and a thumbs up, I said that yes I was. We discussed when I could start, and I suggested sometime in June as I had to hand in my notice and prepare the move. He agreed and said that he'd post off to me the paperwork including a breakdown of my salary. Lying in bed on the Saturday morning, Martin and I couldn't believe our eyes on seeing just how much my salary would be. That night, we went to the Grosvenor and had a whale of a time.

Over the next few weeks there was an awful lot to be done. Martin left his post at the school with little regret, and we set about arranging for our furniture to go into storage. Much to Martin's parents' shock, he announced to them our departure within the next few weeks. I don't think that his mother liked me very much that day. I had a good send off in the pub from the lads at the bank, and was handed a good wad of cash to help us on our way. As I said my farewells I felt an overwhelming sadness in a way. How far I'd come in five short years. From been thrown out of the army, meeting the love of my life, and landing a job with one of the most prestigious banks in the world, to a new life in Luxembourg. I felt very blessed indeed. On the morning of 12 June 1980, Martin and I sat looking around at our home of the past few years. I could tell that Martin, who'd lived there before I came along, was filled with great sadness and my heart went out to him. We had spent some happy times together there and I prayed to God that we'd made the right decision, because there was to be no going back.

When I think of the events of that day thirty-four years ago, I often wonder if we had known what was to be a quite difficult couple of years for us, whether we would have had enough courage to leave. Martin had left his secure job as a teacher, admittedly a job that he was never very happy in, to face life in Luxembourg without even having any work to go to. And as for myself, I'd given up a job that many men would die for. At the time, all of us working at the bank thought that we had a job for life, and so was I being very wise? As it happens, in the mid-1980s, the Birmingham branch was closed down and all of the security men were made redundant. They received a good compensation package and the bank paid off their mortgages, but they'd never find another job of the calibre of the one that they'd just lost. So I can count my self fortunate. Martin was to be unemployed for our first two years in Luxembourg, financially this wasn't a problem as my salary was excellent, but I did worry that he'd become unhappy and bored. Don't forget that back then, we had no rights as a gay couple, and while the court knew about him, as I made no secret of our relationship, I was still regarded as being a single man, and Martin had no status in law. I was so worried about this that I took out a large life insurance policy with him as beneficiary. If I were to die of natural causes or accidental death, he would at least be taken care of. After saying all of that, we were very happy and Martin has said a thousand times since then that he never once regretted our move. Things of course did get better for him. He was offered a job with a large company of lawyers. Martin did now have a good job, and equally as importantly, a Luxembourg ID card which gave him legitimacy. He was later offered a very good job by a young English lawyer. This chap thought a lot of Martin and was quick to snap him up when he finally left his previous employers. Martin was much happier in his new job, and spent a few years working and doing something that he really enjoyed. His chance came when he sat a competition for an English language proofreader in 1989 at the European Parliament. He passed and started there in October of that year, nine years after we'd first left England. Now, both European civil servants, our lives were complete.

It was about this time that I finally stopped drinking for good. While I'd never drunk to the extent that I had in the army, I still drank far too much. My health really started to suffer and I knew in my heart that if I were to continue, then I risked losing the person that I valued more than my own life. And so I stopped, and have never touched a drop since. Towards the end of the 1980s, our lives became so ordinary and unremarkable that we could truly be described as 'respectable homosexuals.' Our lifestyle mirrored that of our heterosexual friends with no differences except the obvious one. From time to time we had the odd foray out into the gay scene both in Luxembourg and further afield, but as we got older this too diminished. I immersed myself in music doing something that I loved and playing with various musical combinations including orchestra, wind band, pit orchestra, and chamber music. In 2001 I was became seriously ill and eventually retired on the grounds of invalidity. Martin was unable to retire until he reached fifty-five and I occupied my time by first writing my autobiography, and then a history of the Spencer and Jackson families. Once Martin had retired, we first settled in a provincial French town called Rochefort, later moving to Bordeaux where I was diagnosed with throat cancer. It was then that we finally decided to return to the country of our birth after an absence of thirty years where we bought a small house in the delightful, Cotswold village of Broadway. I think that I can honestly say that I've led an eventful life, a life that I always divide into two, pre-1975 and, post-1975. And although the events at Bassingbourne were traumatic for me, leaving the army when I did changed my life for the better forever.

13

The End of a Very Long Letter

I will go to my grave, John and Bill, saying that the Labouchere Amendment of, August 7 1885, stained the reputation of a parliament that called itself the jewel in the crown of democracy, forever. At the stroke of a pen in the early hours of the morning, this petty piece of vindictive, and unjust legislation, criminalised a large swathe of Englishmen both then, and for generations to come for no other reason than that they were 'different'. Huge numbers of these same men, fought and sacrificed their lives in the service of their country in two world wars, and countless other conflicts around the world. But had their sexual orientation been known, their actions would have counted for nothing in the eyes of the law. Men like myself, who spent most of our waking hours fearing discovery and forever having to look over our shoulders, and never being allowed to be our real selves by the state. Men who faced public humiliation and hatred, forever branded as 'queer', and a danger to society. They were victims of blackmail, often sentenced to two years imprisonment, being forever branded with a criminal record. What exactly for?

Whenever I talk to young people on the subject of homosexuality, I invariably tell them the story of Alan Turing. Turing was the father of the modern computer and the genius who cracked the German 'Enigma' code. By doing this he saved the lives of countless thousands of human beings. His actions are thought to have shortened the Second World War by at least two years, and what were the rewards heaped on him by a grateful British nation? Nothing! Why? Because Alan Touring was a poof, a Nancy boy, a shirt-lifter, or one of the many other filthy names given to men like him by an uncaring and hateful society. No honours for a *man like him*, no library buildings named after a *man like him*, no statues erected in public squares for a *man like him*.

A short time after the end of the war, Alan Turing was arrested for homosexual offences. He'd been caught out after having a loving relationship with another man. Taken before the courts he was given the option of chemical castration, yes, chemical castration, or two years in prison. He opted for castration. A few years later Alan Turing killed himself. When I tell the young this story, often I don't think that they believe me, but every word of it is the truth. Not long ago in 2013, the Queen granted Turing a posthumous Royal Pardon. Very nice of her, but as the brave campaigner for gay rights, Peter Tatchel, says, 'What of the countless thousands of other men who were charged under the same laws?' No pardons for them it seems. And I count myself as being one of these men myself. It saddens me that by far the most homophobic members of British society today are the men and women of our generation, John and Bill. Perhaps understandable given that we were born into, and were bought up in a society that hated men like me, men who were not '*normal.* '

I often say that as we can't turn back the clock, then perhaps we shouldn't look back at history, but I do find it so difficult sometimes. Since the partial-decriminalisation of homosexual acts in 1967, there have been a number of amendments to the sexual offences bill. In 1994, the age of homosexual consent was lowered to eighteen. In 2000, it was lowered again to sixteen to bring it into line with the heterosexual age of consent. The sexual offences act of 2003, deleted the offences of gross indecency and buggery from statuary law and sexual activity between more than two men is no longer illegal.

Homosexuality within the armed forces was finally decriminalised in the armed forces in 2000, thanks largely to a ruling by the Court of Human Rights. Gay men and women were allowed the rights of 'Civil Partnerships' in 2005 and since March of this year, 2014, gay men and women are now allowed to legally marry in a registry office.

If anyone had said to me back in 1975, that any of the above amendments would happen, I would have laughed in their faces and said, 'Not within my lifetime.' I'm more than happy to admit that I've been proved wrong.

Ten years ago, at the conclusion of a filmed interview that I did for a group called 'Before Stonewall', I said the following: 'We, as gay men and women should never take for granted the huge freedoms that we've gained in recent years, as there are many in British society who would like to put us all back in the closet, lock the door, and throw away the key ... or worse.' That is as true today as it was then. We live in an increasingly violent, hostile, and hate-filled world, and as the lessons of history have taught us, minority groups, who are seen as somehow 'different', make very easy targets.

Well, Bill and John, that brings the longest letter of my life to its close. I hope that you've found its contents both informative, and illuminating, and if it's increased your knowledge by just a fraction, then I'll feel that I've done what I set out to do. Thanks for being so patient.

With my very best wishes, and may God go with you both.

David

Broadway, 28 August 2014

14
John's Reply ... and My Reply to John

Dear Dave,

Thank you for your very long letter, in the form of your book, to Bill Coughlan and me. You asked me to reply so that my response could be printed with the book. I shall be brief.

I thought your account was a brilliant summary of the wider picture both old and new: fluent writing, always moving forward, and very informative. I found the first part particularly illuminating, most of it previously not known to me, nor, I suspect, to many people. And, of course, the reporting of your own circumstances and difficulties were of great personal interest to me because of my own military music background plus my Civil Service experience. I felt a sense of relief as you then took the reader through the various stages and aspects of reform, both social and legal. From my own memory of the infamous Profumo Affair, it seems to me that it must have had the effect of holding up some of the changes to some extent; since it was said to have brought down the Government of the day (see Bringing the House Down by David Profumo), I think the Establishment must have been very nervous about any of relaxation of the law and practice of the time.

Finally, and Bill has also remarked on this, I do not understand why the specialist clubs and other facilities continue to exist. I would have thought that total integration would have been the aim and any segregation now unwelcome. If it is of any help, you might like to know that in my own specialist field of Equality in Education and Employment, my views are just the same, even to the extent of questioning the ultimate value of the Paralympic Games.

Congratulations on producing an excellent piece of writing of a valuable document.

With very best wishes,

John

29 September 2014

Dear John,

Very many thanks for your kind comments on my book. I would imagine that the first half of the letter was indeed illuminating for a man of your generation. I did endeavour to highlight the various aspects of reform over the years, as you say. No one is more aware than I that although you can change laws at the stroke of a pen, changing a society's attitude takes very much longer, often generations. This explains the phenomenal rise of gay venues after 1967, and does most certainly have a lot to do with 'equality'. Almost as a body, homosexuals with their new found freedoms quickly started to 'flex their muscles', and saw no reason why we should give huge amounts of our money to businesses who largely despised us, hence the rapid rise of gay-owned venues. It seemed to us that these straight businesses were quite happy to take our money but not to offer us 'equal' treatment alongside their heterosexual clientèle. Not only were the new gay-owned businesses highly successful for the owners, but gave a great deal of satisfaction to their gay clients who wanted to give a two-fingered salute to the many who still saw us as 'perverts'. The revenue generated by gay-owned enterprises quickly became known in wider circles as the power of 'the pink pound', and the owners of largely 'straight' venues began to realize that they were losing vast amounts of money from a very large potential client base.

It's also no great surprise that largely left-wing gay liberation movements sprang up and came to prominence in the early seventies. Once the closet door had been opened, then there was no closing it again, and these groups, the forerunners of 'Outrage', played a huge part in forcing greater change for homosexuals' rights. They played a significant part in the rapid changes in the law that followed over the next few years. Change has indeed come, but has taken a very long time. Most people today, perhaps with the exception of many of our generation, are far more open and accepting of gay men and women. In fact, I find that today's young are fascinated by the many stories that gay men like myself can tell them of the dark days prior to 1967.

I would like to comment on the last paragraph of your letter, though. I think that both you and Bill have missed the point completely with your comments about gay clubs and bars. While the exclusive gay hotel is now almost extinct, the vibrant gay social venues are still thriving and will continue to do so. This has nothing to do with equality, and everything to do with sexual preference. Just like their heterosexual counterparts, young gay men go out on the town in search of 'romance', and hopefully much more, something that they're unlikely to find by going to largely heterosexual clubs and disco's. Although of a different generation to today's young people, as a gay man myself and in the past, a regular user of gay clubs and bars, I can perfectly well understand the need for such venues. Of course, it doesn't always come down to sex, but often does, and socialising with other gay people, people who understand you and your needs and feelings, is equally as important today as it's ever been. As I say, it's not about 'equality', in this instance, but 'sexuality'. After all, if you're a lover of classical music, you wouldn't join a jazz club, would you?

Once again, John, may I thank you for your kind comments on the book/letter. It was my many conversations with you and Bill that inspired me to write it in the first place, and I'll always be grateful to you both. Although it may never be widely read, it will most certainly end up in some important libraries and archives within the UK, and who knows, may well be read by future generations who will possibly wonder what the fuss was all about.

With my best wishes as always,

Dave

Broadway, 30 September 2014